Wind

and

Wave

Wind and Wave

and

Wave

Sea Tales From Around Our Coast

Robert C. Parsons

CREATIVE PUBLISHERS

St. John's, Newfoundland and Labrador
2003

Le Conseil des Arts | The Canada Council
du Canada | for the Arts

We acknowledge the support of The Canada Council for the Arts for our
publishing program.

We acknowledge the financial support of the Government of Canada through the
Book Publishing Industry Development Program (BPIDP) for our
publishing program.

∞ Printed on acid-free paper

Published by
CREATIVE PUBLISHERS
an imprint of CREATIVE BOOK PUBLISHING
a division of Creative Printers and Publishers Limited
a Print Atlantic associated company
P.O. Box 8660, St. John's, Newfoundland and Labrador A1B 3T7

First Edition
Typeset in 11 point Bookman

Printed in Canada by:
PRINT ATLANTIC

National Library of Canada Cataloguing in Publication

ISBN 1-894294-62-9
Parsons, Robert Charles, 1944-
    Wind and wave : sea tales from around our coast / Robert C. Parsons. -- 1st ed.

Includes bibliographical references and index.
ISBN 1-894294-62-9

    1. Navigation--Newfoundland--History. 2. Shipwrecks--Newfoundland. 3.
Seafaring life--Newfoundland. 4. Ships--Newfoundland. I. Title.

FC2170.S5P375 2003   F1122 P37 2003 971.8   C2003-902979-4
F1122.P37 2003

TABLE OF CONTENTS

ACKNOWLEDGEMENTS

With such a proliferation of material and images in this electronic age, the problem of proper copyright is compounded. Yet I have made every effort to identify, credit appropriately, and obtain publication rights from copyright holders of illustrations and photos in this book. Notice of any errors or omissions in this regard will gratefully be received and corrections made in any subsequent edition.

I give my personal acknowledgement and appreciation to those who sent me information or directed me to a story. I say a hearty thank you. Your names are listed in the sources at the end of *Wind and Wave: Sea Tales from Around Our Coast*. Over the years, several who read my stories in various books wrote to say they appreciated the index in a non-fiction book. Finding the page number references to a town, ship or person was, naturally, much easier than thumbing and searching through pages. Thus, in the view of saving space, book length and costs, *Wind and Wave* has two indices and no story sources. Anyone who wishes sources where I found the information on a particular tale, can contact me at the address below.

Readers will notice that Chapter 19, The Memory of *Little Jap*, is footnoted and illustrates, to a certain degree, the original sources for a story.

I would also like to thank the Newfoundland and Labrador Arts Council which provided financial help for the research and writing of this book.

Robert C. Parsons
32 Pearson Place
Grand Bank, NL
A0E 1W0
E-mail: robert.parsons2@nf.sympatico.ca
Website: http://shipwrecks.nf.ca
May 2003

AUTHOR'S NOTES AND INTRODUCTION

"PRESERVING NEWFOUNDLAND AND LABRADOR'S MARITIME HISTORY, ONE TALE AT A TIME"

Often I get asked, Where do you get the stories and is there any end to Newfoundland and Labrador's sea tales? I'm beginning to think there is no end; perhaps we haven't yet scratched the surface of the accounts and narratives which relate the heroism and sacrifice of our seafaring ancestors.

All stories in *Wind and Wave: Sea Tales From Around Our Coast* are new and different, but a shorter version of the first chapter — the loss of *Sailor's Home* — was recounted in my first book *Lost at Sea*. Back then I only had a folk song to flesh out the details. Since that time, I located the crew list and a version of the story told from a different perspective; that of the words of a survivor of the wreck of *Sailor's Home*. His story, I felt, was so unique and told from another perspective that I had to present it here for you in *Wind and Wave*.

I'd like to think in this book, as well, I have located and written about vessels from Newfoundland and Labrador communities that are not as well known for shipping and marine misadventures. Often the larger centers with its ship fleets, both past and present, get more attention. But the smaller towns played a vital role in the era of the sailing ship — many vessels were built and owned in towns of less than 500 people. When its ships and crew were lost, these towns, on a per capita basis, were dealt devastating setbacks in terms of human resources, economic and financial losses. Thus in *Wind and Wave* are ship stories from towns like St. Jones Within, Point La Haye, The Rams, Harry's Harbour, Charleston, Green's Harbour and many more.

Another point. I made up my mind long ago to follow one cardinal rule in all my writing — to try to be as *clear* as possible. I have given up any thought or hope of writing poetically or symbolically (whatever that is), or in any style that might win me a Pulitzer Prize. I also can't, or won't, write footnoted versions that would raise my profile in the eyes of academic scholars. As you, good reader, may have gathered, I write for the people — those who are descendants of our hardy fishermen and those who love a yarn from the sea. Don't let the word "yarn" mislead anyone; each story within this book is true.

My stories don't write themselves. I usually have to go into archives, read old papers, talk to corespondents and piece the story together bit by bit, often by combining several different sources. Sometimes a sea story may linger for a year or two before I'm satisfied I can't get any other relevant information. But often "you have to go with what you have" and, even though certain details, crew lists (which I try to present in every story) and ship statistics are not available, then I have no choice but give you a shorter version. I hope you'll forgive me. I don't think you, the reader, will have trouble with this, but since we are all friends, I thought I would let you know.

How does *Wind and Wave* fit into a pattern of books of the sea? Here's a brief summary of publication dates, style and theme of my earlier books:

1. **Lost at Sea Volume I**, 1991. Ranges from 1868 to 1925 with stories mainly from the Burin Peninsula, but especially Grand Bank.

2. **Lost at Sea Volume II**, 1992. Ranges from 1925 to 1977 with stories mainly from the

Burin Peninsula, but especially Grand Bank. In 2001, both these books above were combined to form *Lost at Sea: A Compilation.*

3. **Wake of the Schooners**,1993. Stories of shipwrecks from the Newfoundland's South Coast from 1857 to 1977.

4. **Toll of the Sea: Stories from the Forgotten Coast**, 1995. Marine tales of twenty-nine communities from Red Island, Placentia Bay to Port aux Basques.

5. **Vignettes of a Small Town**, 1997. Historical pieces from Grand Bank.

6. **Survive the Savage Sea: Tales from Our Ocean Heritage**,1998. Stories from all around Newfoundland's coast beginning at Highlands on the west coast right around to McDougall's Gulch.

7. **Committed to the Deep: Stories and Memoirs,** 1999. Thirty-nine stories; many taken from interviews and first-person accounts of seamen, rescuers, captains, shipowners and land-based relatives.

8. **Raging Winds . . . Roaring Sea**, 2000. Tales from all over Newfoundland and Labrador. Story introductions explain where the ideas for stories begin or where research originates.

9. **In Peril on the Sea: Shipwrecks of Nova Scotia**, 2000. Sea tales from our maritime neighbor to the west. Stories arranged chrono-logically from 1873 to 1972.

If I had to catagorize *Wind and Wave* I would have to say it is most like number 6 in that the stories are arranged geographically. This collection begins with Fortune on the tip of the Burin Peninsula and continues around the coast clockwise to encompass virtually every shoreline of our province. As a passing note I might add, for those who like to know such things, that the last story written was of the disappearance of *Beverley*. The account, a more personal tale, came from the reports from the court of inquiry (weeks of court work and thousands of words reduced in this book to a reasonable length) investigating the disappearance of the S.S. *Beverley*, Chapter 39.

That's it then. Now let's step back in time and travel together to see in word and image how our seafaring peoples made their way along the vast expanse of the Atlantic that surrounds our province.

Chapter 1

A Survivor's Story

The loss of the schooner *Sailor's Home* was a disaster that combined the classic elements of the sea: a violent storm, a wreck on a desolate landscape, and survivors who barely escaped death by inching up over a steep icy cliff. Of the five crew — Captain Thomas Bennett, mate Philip Elford, cook Benjamin Miles, seamen George Tom Hines and Samuel Major, all of Fortune — three returned, one of whom, Elford, recorded the last hours of *Sailor's Home*.

John Lake, a businessman of Fortune, built the fifty-seven-ton *Sailor's Home* at Fortune. Not much is written about the vessel's long sea career, but it is known it survived the devastating gale of 1887 when Philip Lake was captain. By 1890, the ship was twenty-six years old and had gone through many storms. However, in the end the rocks of Miquelon claimed it. One of the survivors, Philip Elford, wrote of the final hours of *Sailor's Home* and recalled:

> We left Sydney on Monday morning of December 1, 1890, bound for St. Pierre with a cargo of coal. The wind was moderate. At 8 p.m. as the wind increased, we lowered the sails and reefed them. At 4 a.m. December 2, we hove to under a reefed foresail until daylight. By eight that night the wind veered to the

north-northwest, blowing a gale and with a thick snow storm.

Our foreboom broke and the foresail split in two. We lowered the storm sail and ran before the wind and sea until 11 p.m. The *Sailor's Home* strained a great deal with the heavy seas continually breaking over the decks and it began to leak considerably.

For sailors, even during the worst ocean storms, there is no lingering below deck, avoiding duties or lying in bunk. The crew, especially the deckhands, had to continue their work on deck, climb the rigging, raising or lowering sail, reef or tie it, and generally handle and manoeuver the sailing ship. As heavy seas rose and broke across deck, they held on or used life lines to secure themselves against the ever present dangers.

Without any coal supplies on the island, Newfoundland ships and men had to travel to Nova Scotia to obtain supplies. Scores of ships were lost in the coal trade. This ad of 1891, in the same time period *Sailor's Home* was lost, lists the schooners which brought coal and the St. John's business, P. & L. Tessier, which sold it.

Up to the 1940s, when wheelhouses were built on deck, the wheel was exposed to the elements and often men were tied or lashed to the wheel. Aboard *Sailor's Home*, Mate Elford stood to the wheel and later, after it was all over, described what happened next:

> I was at the helm when a very heavy sea broke over the ship washing me overboard, but I fortunately

caught the boom tackle. The next lurch of the schooner landed me back on board again. The same sea broke into the binnacle (housing or covering for the compass) and destroyed the compass.

Captain Bennett took the wheel while I went below to change my clothes. Having done so in haste, I was just coming on deck when a tremendous sea broke over the ship, carrying overboard the captain, cook and even the wheel itself. Not seeing anyone on deck, I first thought that I was the only one left on board, but the next moment I noticed the cook, Benjamin Miles, clinging to one of the stern davits which was hanging in the water.

I threw him a rope which he grabbed, but I could not haul him on board. After awhile he became exhausted and let go. There was no sign of the captain whatsoever. I next found two other members of the crew who had barely saved themselves by clinging to the rigging.

Now three men had to do the work of five: try to stabilize the ship, effect repairs, man the pumps, and handle sail. Perhaps under ideal sailing conditions they may have been able to do so, but a violent storm raged around them. With the wheel gone, it was near impossible to keep the ship into the wind. Seeing two of their crew and close friends swept to their death was disheartening, but it also made them more careful while working on deck. Elford continued his story:

At this time it was snowing heavily with a storm of wind. We let *Sailor's Home* drive until noon the next day. By the next Monday night and all day Tuesday we were busy trying to get the water out of the vessel, but the pumps choked. We were forced to break through the forecastle floor and bail water out that way.

About midnight on Tuesday (December 8) the vessel struck broadside against a cliff close to

Miquelon Head. One of the others jumped ashore on a crag. *Sailor's Home* went off with the sea and was again hove against the cliff when a second man jumped. On the third wave the third man reached the crag.

The space on the rock to which we were clinging was so small we had to hold on to each other to keep from slipping off. The cliff above us was partially covered with ice and it was extremely cold and snowing all the time.

Sailor's Home, after striking against the cliff three times, bounded off a short distance, capsized and sank.

Their little vessel and two crew mates were gone. Three men — Elford, Hines, and Major — clung precariously to a crag swept by seas in the dead of a winter storm. They knew they were on Cap Miquelon, at the northernmost tip of the French Islands of St. Pierre and Miquelon. Cap Miquelon is described in the September 1967 edition of *National Geographic Magazine* as isolated, bleak, and high, with granite cliffs rising 500 feet out of a deep sea. *National Geographic* says that it was "A terrible place to be shipwrecked. How could anyone be rescued there?" Elford remembered:

Loss of the Sailor's Home
Verses 13 to 18

Sailor's Home was in the breakers,
All with a dismal shock,
When we three after each other,
Jumped out upon a rock.

The mountain seemed so lofty,
Our feet and fingers stiff,
We thought it was only vanity,
To try and scale the cliff.

But the stoutest man among us,
Against the cliff stood tight,
Another man on his shoulders,
Got up on top all right.

He then lowered down a scravit,
He tied another on,
And we two made an effort,
To get up to the other man.

As last we all got up there,
Out in the drifting snow,
We started for the country,
But where we did not know.

The walking it was awful,
The snow was up to our knees,
We thought we'd have to give up,
And lay down there and freeze.

The next morning we commenced trying to get further up the precipice to the level on top. We were so weak and cold we made slow progress and did not reach the top until four in the afternoon. About dusk, we found a fisherman's hut at a distance of one and a half miles away from the cliff top and remained there for the night.

As with many Newfoundland disasters, the local folksinger/poet composed a poem or ditty summarizing the event. The folk song *The Loss of the Sailor's Home* describes how the three exhausted men scaled the cliff — a mountain in the words of the three who climbed it — that appeared so lofty it seemed "only vanity to try and scale that cliff."

Each man was exhausted; fingers and feet were stiff with cold. But the heaviest man of the three stood pressed against the side of the rock, while another climbed on his shoulders to reach the higher level. He "lowered down a scravit (deadwood), he tied another man on, and we two made an effort to get up the other man."

According to the poem, in the fisherman's hut they found some fish, a loaf of bread, matches, kindling for a fire, water, a blanket, and some dry clothes. "We then lit up a fire and boiled the kettle too, we drank a cup of coffee which warmed us through and through." Elford also recalled the fight for survival:

> At nine o'clock the next morning, Thomas Hines, who was stronger than the rest since he had changed his wet clothing shortly before the vessel struck, began his walk to Miquelon Town about three miles away.
>
> Hines told the people there of the condition of his shipmates in the hut. The folks at once sent off four men to the assistance of the shipwrecked sailors. They found them badly frostbitten, one of them so bad that he had to be carried. The three survivors of *Sailor's Home* remained at Miquelon for five days under a doctor's care and three more days in the St. Pierre hospital.

Eventually two came to Fortune while the third remained on the French Islands under medical care for a longer time. Elford had two badly frozen feet, Sam Major had hands and feet frozen, but Hines suffered little ill effects.

The memoirs of Philip Elford and the anonymous writer of a folk poem gave us a glimpse into the world of wreck and death at the tip of Miquelon Island. Today one of Captain Bennett's grandchildren, Barbara Bennett Esposito, living in Connecticut, writes of her Newfoundland ancestors who followed the sea.

To this end she says that Captain Bennett was thirty-one years old when he lost his life on the *Sailor's Home* and was married to Amelia Burton. He left twin children: Edward William and Myra. Myra died young, but Edward William emigrated to the United States.

Dorothy O (above) near Rencontre East. For years it was commanded by captains John Ben Francis; then Johnny Rose (inset circa 1945) of Hermitage. *Dorothy O* burned in Hermitage Bay on June 7, 1950. Often a rhyme helped people remember their favourite schooners, like these Belleoram ships: *Antoine C. Santos, Lucy Edwina* and *Dorothy O:*

> *Santos* is the racer, *Lucy* is the same
> *Dorothy O* is very slow, but gets there just the same.

Photos courtesy H. Perkins and the *Atlantic Guardian*

Chapter 2

Noxall and the August Gale of 1927

Belleoram/South Coast

Six men on the Fortune Bay schooner *Noxall* battled the August Gale of 1927 and almost won. It was a fight to the finish, but nature's worst elements prevailed: *Noxall* went down and one of the crew had perished. Yet there is always the unexpected for the outcome may have been different except for a chance collision.

It took days before final reports from outlying towns came in to St. John's, but eventually it was learned that the sudden pounce of the tail end of a hurricane had claimed seven schooners and thirty-six lives.

In late summer, hurricanes, originating near the Tropic of Cancer, lash their way northward devastating parts of the southern United States. By the time these violent winds reach the Maritimes, much of their fury is spent. In the era of sail, there was no long-range forecast to warn the ships and the final winds of the hurricane's blunt force, sweeping across the fishing grounds and into exposed harbours, came suddenly and with deadly results. Locally, these wind storms were called the August (or September) Gales.

For two and a half days, from August 24-27, 1927, when several small schooners were on the fishing grounds, one of the most memorable "August Gales" to ravage the southern part of Newfoundland struck with destructive and deadly results. It is still talked about today by the descendants of the mariners who survived the gale.

Noxall left Sydney with coal in mid-August 1927, bound for Bay de Verde. On the night of Wednesday, August 24, when the gale first pounced, the schooner was off Cape Spear, near St. John's. Most crew — Captain William A. Kearley, Uriah Dicks, Cecil Poole, E. Rose, E. Caines, and Albert Cluett — probably hailed from Fortune Bay although it is known that both Cluett, married with two children, and Captain Kearley were from Belleoram.

Launched at Essex, Massachusetts, in 1901, as a salt fish banker, *James W. Parker* was sold in 1920 to the Kearleys of Belleoram and renamed *Noxall*. It netted ninety-six tons and was 101 feet long, but these dimensions meant little when an August Gale with all its fury struck the ship. On May 28, 1927, it had been apprehended by authorities off Prince Edward Island and held for smuggling liquor. *Noxall* was returned to the owners, but its cargo was seized.

In August 1927, *Noxall* battled the wind and waves, but was cut down by the schooner *Veda McKown* somewhere off Cape Spear. *Veda McKown*, owned by Sainthill's business of Sydney, Nova Scotia, struck *Noxall* somewhere near the port bow. The lookout on *Noxall* barely had time to determine the other schooner's name before it disappeared in the fog.

All Wednesday night, *Noxall*'s crew struggled at the pumps in a determined effort to get their schooner into St. John's. The August Gale increased in intensity and *Noxall* settled lower and lower in the water. About 9 a.m. on Thursday, Albert Cluett, who was at the wheel, was washed overboard and drowned.

Captain Kearley knew it was only a matter of hours before his vessel would sink and ordered his men to get the lifeboat over the side. As they rowed away from *Noxall*'s side, the vessel went down.

A gale raged full in their face and they were driven twenty miles to sea. But between a long pull at the oars, a little shift in the wind, the five survivors reached Flat Rock near Ferryland early Friday, August 26. They were exhausted, but alive. Officials in Flat Rock sent a message to the Minister of Justice and *Noxall's* survivors were taken to St. John's. Dr. Mosdell, the Member of the House of Assembly for Fortune Bay, lodged them in the YMCA building. It is not clear if the schooner *Veda McKown* was later located or held responsible for the collision.

It is known that two years later, on October 21, 1929, the rocky shores of Labrador claimed the schooner *Veda McKown*. It was commanded by Captain George Hardy and had loaded 700 quintals of fish at Harrington, Labrador. A short distance from port the schooner struck a "sunker" or submerged rock near Harrington. With a large hole in the bow just below the waterline, it immediately

An advertisement in the newspaper *Fishermen's Advocate* for the schooner *Veda McKown*, the vessel which struck and sank *Noxall* in 1927. Both ships were built at Essex, Massachusetts. At the time it was offered for sale, *Veda McKown* was moored at Jersey Harbour. The advertisement illustrates how Newfoundland businesses knew about and purchased mainland schooners.

slid off the rock. Realizing he could not return to port with the disabled schooner, Hardy decided to abandon ship and launched the lifeboat. He and his crew of five returned to Harrington. *Veda McKown* lay in forty-five feet of water and was declared a total loss.

Noxall's loss was one of the first reports of the effects of the intense wind storm that raged over Newfoundland in August 1927. Within the next few days, other accounts of disaster trickled into authorities. At Humbermouth on the west coast, a logger, George Hayden, aged forty-nine and married with three children, was blown off a boom of wood and drowned. By Sunday, August 28, the full extent of damage came in from various south coast towns.

Isle aux Morts — Newfoundland's south coast bore the brunt of the August Gale and the loss of ships and lives ranged from westernmost Isle aux Morts to Fox Harbour in the east. Little is known of *Annie Jean* of Isle aux Morts; newspapers of the day carried its name but made little mention of the crew and destination. As far as can be determined, the vessel was on a trip to St. Pierre and four men, including owner/captain Wilson Green, were lost.

Burnt Islands — Next door to Isle aux Morts, the town of Burnt Islands realized after the gale abated that the schooner *Vienna* would not be coming home. It was bound from St. Pierre to Burnt Islands on a fishing voyage. *Vienna*'s crew were the young men of the town: Captain John Chaulk, Freeman Organ, Thomas Keeping, John P. Keeping, and Robert Herritt, who was married. George Strickland from Lapoile also sailed on *Vienna*. Its wreckage drifted into Fox Roost.

Rencontre West — Arthur Durnford's schooner *Effie May* had been under repair at St. Pierre and left for Rencontre West on August 24. Somewhere in the fifty miles separating the French Islands from home port, *Effie May* disappeared with crew: Arthur Durnford, married and age thirty-four, and his two brothers, George and John all of Rencontre West. John's two sons went to St. Pierre for the trip:

Garfield, age twelve and Frank, sixteen. Benjamin Herritt was a deckhand aboard the schooner.

Red Harbour — In Placentia Bay the gale ravaged the fishing fleet. The derelict hull of *John C. Loughlin*, a Red Harbour vessel, was located off Ship Cove, near Argentia. One dead man was found in the rigging — Captain William Albert Loughlin. His brothers Fred and Charles, as well four men from Flat Island or Woody Island, Josiah Barrett, age twenty-four; Gordon Frampton, twenty-four; Herman Peach, twenty-five; and Josiah Stacey, eighteen; were never seen again. The derelict was later salvaged, repaired, and renamed *Velma*, but the owners, realizing the trauma it would cause, did not sail the schooner into Red Harbour again.

Rushoon — On August 15, Danny Cheeseman and his young crew hoisted sail and *Hilda Gertrude* slipped out of Rushoon, bound for the Cape St. Mary's fishing grounds. Its crew: Captain Cheeseman, age around thirty, Patrick Gaulton, twenty-two, and Michael Hann, twenty-two, belonged to Rushoon; John and Michael Norman, Parker's Cove; cook Oliver Dicks, Baine Harbour; and Tommy Hawco of St. Joseph's. Hawco, over fifty years of age, was the eldest. Except for Michael Norman, all were married and several had small children.

Cheeseman and his crew failed to return to their home port of Rushoon — victims of the gale. Two bodies — Dicks and Hawco — were recovered when the derelict *Hilda Gertrude* was found near Placentia.

Fox Harbour — Over the years since it had been built in 1900 in Fox Harbour, *Annie Healy* gained the reputation of being the best fishing schooner in

Placentia Bay. Built and owned by Richard K. Healy who christened the vessel "Annie" for his daughter Annie (Healy) Furlong, it netted thirty-seven tons and was fifty-five feet long. *Annie Healy* had been rebuilt in 1926 under the supervision of James Healy, son of the builder.

On August 25 it was caught out in the sudden storm. The *Telegram* of August 26, 1927, said, "Terrible loss of life in Thursday's storm. Feared not less that thirty-three perished; many vessels wrecked. A schooner reported off Merasheen Bank with a man clinging to the wreckage has disappeared. It probably had a crew of seven men." This vessel was, in all likelihood, *Annie Healey*.

Captain John Mullins carried six crew with him on *Annie Healy*: his son Michael, age seventeen, James King, John Foley, Patrick Bruce, John Kelly and Charles Sampson. All were from Fox Harbour and married except Michael Mullins. Memorial services for the crew were conducted by Father Adrian Dee at Most Holy Rosary Church in Argentia. Eventually Mrs. John Mullins, a widow now with a large family of young children, moved to Corner Brook, a logging town on the opposite side of the island from the fishing town of Fox Harbour.

Several other vessels missing for days finally reported in damaged condition. Three men of Clattice Harbour, John Follett and his two sons, jumped from *Mystery II* as it was driving past Clattice Harbour. One son, Jim, survived, but the father and the other son disappeared. Another man from Clattice Harbour, Joseph Picco, was washed off the deck of *Mary Bernice*, owned by the Lakes of Darby's Harbour. His body was never found.

Other vessels were lost around Newfoundland with no loss of life: *Winnie Pierce*, with 350 quintals of cod, grounded at the Wadham Islands to total loss. S.S. *Philameena* went ashore at Three Rock Cove, Port au

Port; twenty-five small boats were lost at Bonavista and the schooner *Henry Dowden* went ashore at Biscay Bay near Trepassey. Captain Jim Harris of St. Joseph's saw an unidentified boat submerged with both masts gone ten miles south of Maricot Island, Placentia Bay. There were two men clinging to the wreckage and Harris made two attempts at rescue, but was unsuccessful.

Captain James W. Osmond in the schooner *Bretwalda* left Grand Bank on Tuesday, August 23. He met the storm head on by Wednesday. It carried away the foresail, mainsail, jumbo and riding sail as well as the anchors and chain. But Osmond reached Brule in Placentia Bay at 3 p.m. Thursday. He borrowed sails at Harbour Buffett, sailed to Argentia on Sunday where he sent a telegram home to say that he and his crew were safe.

The story of another strange incident in the August Gale of 1927 came from the Collector of Customs at Lamaline. He reported that the schooner *Valena R* drifted in on Morgan's Island, near Lamaline. It was intact with two anchors still in place on the bow, a dory on deck, ten quintals of fish in the hold and, most odd, a lamp still burning in the forecastle. There seemed to be no local knowledge or reports of who owned this ship or where it came from.

From a few items on board, it was determined *Valena R* had recently been in St. Pierre. An examination of fishing records for 1926 showed it belonged to Richard's Harbour/Pushthrough and its captain was William G. Skinner. It was assumed, since no stories of loss of life came from those towns, that the little craft had been driven out of St. Pierre harbour in the storm and that there was no one aboard when it went adrift.

A group of men of Allan's Island and Lamaline led by Maurice Doyle hauled this schooner to a safe anchorage at Allan's Island for the winter. There it was repaired. To the owner's surprise, who thought his vessel had drifted out of St. Pierre and sunk somewhere, word came that he could reclaim *Valena R* at no charge. A truly generous gesture by the residents of Lamaline and Allan's Island in the wake of one of the worst August Gales to ever hit Newfoundland.

Belleoram between 1900 and 1910 with schooners in harbour. Photo Courtesy Rev. Vernon Cluett.

Building of the *Ripple* in Belleoram in 1907; master builder was John Cluett who became known as "Ripple" John. Photo courtesy Rev. Vernon Cluett.

Chapter 3

On the Rocks of St. Shotts: Gordon Stoodley's Story

Jersey Harbour/St. Shotts

In the spring, fog often enshrouds the southern coast of the Avalon peninsula. Fog and ocean currents have been blamed for literally scores of wrecks between St. Shotts and Cape Race. This tale is of one such wreck, Chesley Boyce's schooner *Norma Marilyn*. When it left home port of Jersey Harbour at 7 a.m. on May 1, 1947, heading for the fishing grounds near Cape Race, there was light fog. By the time the vessel arrived off the southern Avalon, fog conditions were, to use a Newfoundland saying, "as thick as pea-soup."

That morning, May 2, the schooner struck the rocks at ·Western Head near St. Shotts. Captain Wilbert Moulton, born in Garnish, carried a south coast crew. Most were from Jersey Harbour and Muddy Hole, a town in Hermitage Bay. Today both towns are abandoned.

Charles Strowbridge was kedgie, but went in a dory when a man became sick or if a dory had only one hand. Gordon Stoodley, doryman on *Norma Marilyn* that spring, recently recalled several aspects of Boyce's banker and its loss.

When launched in Gloucester in 1936, the sixty-four net ton *Norma Marilyn* had a bowsprit. By the early 1940s, when owners installed engines, schooners used less sail. Thus bowsprits, to which the jib and jumbo sails were attached, were removed. As well, without the long and cumbersome sprit, schooners were more maneuverable in narrow, confined harbours. Schooners with no bowsprit were generally termed "knockabouts."

Grandy Brothers ship building and repair yard in Grand Bank

> **Crew of *Norma Marilyn*, Wrecked May 2, 1947, at St. Shotts**
>
> Captain Wilbert Moulton, Garnish
> cook George King, Fortune
> engineer George Sam Welsh, Grand Bank
> mate Chesley Simms, Muddy Hole
> doryman Matt Fudge, Muddy Hole
> doryman Albert "Ted" Morris, Muddy Hole
> doryman Stan Fudge, Muddy Hole
> doryman Bert Griffin, Jersey Harbour
> doryman Gordon Stoodley, Jersey Harbour
> doryman Basil Grandy, Jersey Harbour
> doryman Lloyd Grandy, Jersey Harbour
> doryman Stephen "Tib" Baker, Jersey Harbour
> doryman Freeman Skinner, Jersey Harbour
> doryman/kedgie Charles W. Strowbridge, Red Cove
> doryman Clayton Prior, Sagona Island

removed *Norma Marilyn*'s bowsprit. They then ripped the wood down into plank and made a table for the galley down f'ard — it was such a neat job the top looked like it was constructed out of one piece. Anyone who came aboard had to have a look at "one of the finest tables ever put aboard a schooner."

But the table was not of much use to *Norma Marilyn*'s crew on the morning of May 2. Captain Moulton headed for the Grand Banks and, as was the custom, went along the south coast to take off a course from Cape Race. The compass was working fine. Moulton had taken off the proper course on his chart. But tides along St. Shotts have caused many a careful and experienced captain to lose a ship. Apparently a strong inset of tide pulled the schooner off course in the fog to disastrous results.

Stoodley and his dorymate, Freeman Skinner, had been on watch and were relieved by Ted Morris and Matt Fudge. Stoodley went to his bunk for a nap. He was only there an hour or so, when *Norma Marilyn* struck the base of a cliff at Western Head.

The impact, according to Stoodley, "beat the head off the schooner and that alone would have put it under." But in addition, the foremast struck into the cliff, scrunched along the rock causing rocks and debris to tumble down into the water. With each surge of the schooner from ocean swell, the cross trees caught in the rocks until one last time. The foremast hooked, was pulled up out of its step, and when it went back down probably went through the bottom of the vessel. This was the death blow for *Norma Marilyn*. Soon salt water filled the engine room and stalled the engines forever.

Norma Marilyn leaving North Sydney. Early in its career the schooner carried a bowsprit and had no wheelhouse aft. Photo courtesy of Olive and Bud Boyce, Marystown/Jersey Harbour.

Meanwhile the crew was on deck where a quick survey showed everyone was accounted for and no one injured. The foresail and gaffs had fallen down across the dories on the port side; those four dories were either damaged or hard to get out of the nest. The crew went to the four dories on the starboard side, lifted them out without any problem and put them over the side.

Stoodley knew no one would save their clothes bags even if they could reach them in the bunks below deck. There simply wouldn't be enough room in four dories for fifteen men and all their personal effects. He did think of his new safety razor he bought a few days before. He went to the companionway and attempted to go below, but saw the water sloshing around and knew the razor would go to the bottom off St. Shotts.

As each dory went over the side, some problem did arise. The men were very anxious to get off the schooner as no one knew at what moment it would take its final plunge. More than enough men jumped into the first dory and each subsequent one put over the side had fewer men — overcrowding the first small boat and only one or two men in the last. But that problem was resolved when they leaned to the oars and backed off from the cliff and the ill-fated *Norma Marilyn*. They then divided up four to a dory.

The schooner, which a few minutes before had been their home on the water, sank headfirst, but the sea was not exceptionally deep at the base of the cliff. As they rowed away in the fog, the top of the one mast showed above water and that was the last they saw of *Norma Marilyn*.

Gordon Stoodley recalls that when the crew abandoned the wrecked schooner, he lost one of his new hip rubbers. And what good is one rubber boot? The one he saved, for the right foot, he gave to Maurice Myles in Jersey Harbour. Maurice had one leg and Stoodley's boot fitted perfectly.

St. Shotts was not far away and they pulled into the beach in the town. The tidewaiter for the area, Maun Winsor who was also the wreck commissioner, arranged transportation for the stranded men. He hired a truck to take them to St. John's where they connected with the coastal steamer S.S. *Home* westbound along south coast ports.

When the story appeared in print in the local papers a day or so after the wreck, the heading read **Schooner Total Wreck at St. Shotts**, but said little of the experiences of the crew and how they survived on a coast noted for its wrecks and fatalities.

> The schooner *Norma Marilyn*, owned by Chesley
> Boyce of Jersey Harbour, Moulton master, has gone
> ashore at St. Shotts and is a total loss. The crew have
> landed safely. The vessel, which was seventy-seven
> tons net, was powered by a diesel engine and was
> insured with the Western Marine Insurance Company.

When owner Boyce lost *Norma Marilyn* he had to
search around for a replacement. In Carbonear he chartered the *F & E Adams* which had a Kelvin engine. The
old engine went in fits and starts and was nothing but
trouble for engineer George Sam Welsh. Welsh said to
Captain Moulton that if he bought a schooner with a
Kelvin engine, "don't call me to go with you." Boyce used
F & E Adams for one summer and then purchased the
banker *Jenny Elizabeth*. It did have a Kelvin and Welsh
found work elsewhere.

Stoodley recalls they did well in the Carbonear
schooner. Boyce would have bought it, but the owner was
asking for 42,000 dollars. In the spring of 1948, Chesley
Boyce purchased Petites' *Jenny Elizabeth*. Gordon
Stoodley recalls with a smile that Petites "gave the
schooner away." It was so old, no one wanted to go to sea
on the vessel and as a result, Boyce paid very little for it.
Considering the usual wages he had been getting, Stoodley
again did well — 1,200 dollars for the fishing voyages on
Jenny Elizabeth during the first summer and 1,100 dollars the second.

After that Gordon Stoodley went to Lunenburg, Nova
Scotia, on the bankers. He remembers the higher pay and
the better quality life on the "Lunenburgers" with skippers
like Harry Oxner. He stayed with them five years.

He said to dory mate Freeman Skinner on the first day
of work, "What kind of breakfast did you have?" Skinner
could scarcely contain his excitement on seeing two con-
tainers of milk and two boxes of Corn Flakes on the table,
plus the cook fried up bacon and eggs. It was not the kind
of grub they were used to while on the Newfoundland
schooners and there was plenty of it.

Eventually, as the salt fishery phased out, he found employment on Nova Scotian scallop boats where the pay was good. "But," Gordon says, "there's always a down side for it meant being away from home, Jersey Harbour, for much of the year."

Today he recalls the wreck of *Norma Marilyn* on the rocks of St. Shotts and thanks Divine Providence there was no wind that day, for if it had been windy maybe his story would have been different.

Another wreck at St. Shotts. The S.S. *Crewe* grounded there on June 29, 1901. By the time this photo was taken in 1955, only pieces of the bow section remained. Photo courtesy of Bruce Neal.

Chapter 4

What Happened in Mid-Ocean?

Jersey Harbour/Mid-Atlantic

In June 1927, the *New York Times* newspaper reported an unusual incident on the sea involving a mysterious schooner and a large American steamship. As it turned out the event was unique for the Americans, but no big deal for the Newfoundlanders aboard the schooner.

Liner *American Trader* prepared to sail on its return journey to Plymouth, England, but just before it did, reporters for the *New York Times* asked Captain Theodore Van Beek for his story. Van Beek began his tale, saying that his liner was "en route to New York when on Tuesday, June 21, the first officer on watch, Edward Richmond, called me from below."

It was 5 a.m. Dawn was breaking over the broad Atlantic. *American Trader*'s global position was latitude 47.40 North, longitude 37.35 West. This would put the oceanic liner about

Mysterious Vessel Adrift in Midocean

Spoken to by Liner, Two Men Appear on Deck and Decline Offer of Assistance. "Marjorie and Eileen" Is of Newfoundland Register

"Close encounter with the strange kind" as the papers of the day saw it. It was nothing unusual for Newfoundland sailors.

1,000 miles from the fishing banks and 720 miles from the nearest point of the Irish coast. Officers on the steamer sighted what they termed a "bald-headed" schooner riding the swells directly ahead.

The schooner was eight miles ahead and seemed out of control, bobbing, surging and drifting with the wind and seas. Both men thought something was wrong with the little craft out in the middle of nowhere. Captain Van Beek ordered the engine slowed and nudged his great liner near the schooner.

American Trader (above) was built as Marne in 1920 in the United States and renamed *American Trader* in 1924. Although primarily a freighter, it had passenger accommodations. It was torpedoed and sunk in 1940. Photo courtesy Hubert Hall, SHIPSEARCH Marine.

There seemed to be no sign of life aboard which the captain expected since it seemed to be obviously abandoned. Allowing the great liner to drift as near the wallowing schooner as possible, he could make out the name *Marjorie and Eileen* on the bow. Its rig and structure marked it as a Gloucester or Nova Scotian fishing schooner. Van Beek thought it was far from home like a lost puppy. Perhaps if he tried he could gently nudge or ram the vessel, open a few seams and it would sink. That would eliminate a possible drifting hazard on the ocean.

As he drew near, the captain took a megaphone to hail the schooner in case someone might be alive on it. After calling several times, Captain Van Beek was about to give up when a man came through the schooner's hatchway with a surprised look on his face. He called below and another man with an equal quizzical face came up to look at the immense liner towering above them. To the men on the schooner, the ship seemed to have appeared out of nowhere to be now positioned and stopped by their side.

Captain Van Beek and other crew of *American Trader* who had gathered at the liner's rail could now see the schooner plainly and noted *Marjorie and Eileen* appeared to be in good condition and was actually in no trouble at all on the high seas. Yet its position in mid-ocean troubled him.

He called out, "What's the trouble? Do you need assistance or supplies?"

One of the men on *Marjorie and Eileen* replied, "No trouble. We don't need anything!"

Several moments passed without any conversation. Both crews seemed to be astounded at each other's presence. Finally someone on *Marjorie and Eileen* called out, "We're just drifting along." To close the conversation they went below deck.

"Just drifting along" was obvious to Van Beek. What he couldn't figure out was "Why?" There was nothing else to be done, so he signalled AHEAD to the engine room and *American Trader* moved slowly away.

In the first week in July 1927, *American Trader* docked in New York; the captain told others of his curious meeting on the high seas with a banking schooner so far from the fishing grounds. New York officials asked him to speculate on what the schooner was doing, but Van Beek was at a loss to explain. He could only say it seemed to be of no good purpose.

This ended the story as it appeared in the New York papers. One can only speculate that probably captains of the great liners, specifically Van Beek and *American*

Trader, and newspaper reporters in New York did not realise the purpose and range of sturdy Newfoundland schooners. Nor did they know of the seamanship and great journeys undertaken by Newfoundland seamen. Between 1900 and 1940, the approximate 6,000 mile round trip to Europe and back was routine for Newfoundland schooners, especially those of the south coast.

Although designed as bank fishing schooners, often these vessels were used in the foreign trade to carry fish to Europe and return with salt. In his years as captain of ocean liners, Van Beek had sighted Gloucester and Nova Scotian bankers pursuing their work on the Grand Banks, but had never encountered one in the middle of the ocean.

Van Beek was right about the look and rig of the schooner being of the American type. Although the 105-ton *Marjorie and Eileen*, registered in St. John's, Newfoundland, was owned by Chesley Boyce and Sons of Jersey Harbour, it had been built in Essex, Massachusetts, in 1904 as the *Cavalier*. It measured 105 feet long and twenty-five feet wide. When Boyce purchased the schooner he renamed it after his two nieces.

At the time of its encounter with a "green" captain, *Marjorie and Eileen* was probably becalmed, awaiting winds and just drifting along. The south coast crew had sufficient supplies, needed no help, knew what they were doing and where they were going — Europe with dry fish.

Five years later the stalwart schooner met its doom on the cobblestone strand of Anse a Rodrigue Beach in inner St. Pierre harbour. On August 10, 1932, a storm drove *Marjorie and Eileen* ashore to total wreck. It was in ballast and bound for Sydney, Nova Scotia, to load coal — Captain George Yarn and his crew escaped without injury. Two other south coast schooners were wrecked the same day nearly side by side with *Marjorie and Eileen*: *Admiral Dewey*, owned by Thomas Hardy of Jersey Harbour, and the *Clara F*, owned by the Monroes of St. John's and skippered by Captain Harold Ayres of Fortune.

Chapter 5

A Renown Loss

Burgeo/Rose Blanche/Petites

Burgeo, from the time of its first settlers, has always had enterprises that "did business in great waters" and the town was a choice location for several fishing firms that owned foreign-going vessels. As with any town that sends a fleet of ships to the sea, Burgeo paid its wages in lost ships and seamen. Herein are three tales: one of a tern schooner that disappeared relatively close to home; the other two of schooners that sank in mid-ocean and their crews returned home to sail again.

One of the first Burgeo schooners to disappear with crew was the *Grace Hall*, owned by Clement and Company. Over the years, ten other vessels with Burgeo connections were lost with their entire compliment including: *Dannie Goodwin*, *Heroine*, *Elsie Burdette*, *County of Richmond*, *Beatrice Beck*, and, as recently as 1977, the dragger *Cape Royal*. Another mystery of the sea is the schooner *Ivanhoe*. Little is known of the tern except that it never returned from one of its journeys.

Over the years, over twenty terns, or three masters as they were termed locally, ranging in size from 100 to over 300 tons, were registered to either Thomas, Robert or J.T. Moulton of Burgeo. The 100-ton *Ivanhoe*, one of the first terns owned on the South Coast, was purchased in late 1904 by Thomas Moulton.

By the spring of 1905, *Ivanhoe*, commanded by Nathan Poole of Burnt Islands, was engaged in the fish exporting business and had been to the European ports of Oporto and Lisbon. Poole had a veteran crew with him who all belonged to Burgeo and area: mate Charles Le Roux, cook William Hann, and seamen John Le Roux, William Timbury, and John Newal. Two crew were married.

In late April, *Ivanhoe* loaded salt at Harbour Breton, a town approximately ninety miles east of Burgeo, and sailed for home. From that point on, there was no news it had reached any port, and the ship was never seen again. That spring off Newfoundland's south coast, icebergs were numerous and many believed *Ivanhoe* may have struck one while sailing at night.

Other Burgeo schooners ran into difficulty, but rescue arrived in time. In one such incident, on August 13, 1911, the *Renown* left Burgeo to carry fish to Oporto. The schooner, owned by the Halifax-based Crosbie business, was chartered to Robert Moulton's business. The crew hailed from Burgeo and area: Captain Pennell, mate James McDonald, seamen James Courtney, Arthur Barter, William Swift, and cook J. King. In later years, Arthur Barter sailed on the tern *Duchess of Cornwall* which was intercepted and sunk by a German raider in December 1916. Barter and his crew mates spent two years in a German POW camp before they were released.

Renown had a smooth and uneventful trip eastward and sailed across the Atlantic in sixteen days, but the voyage back to Newfoundland was not so pleasant. After cargo was discharged *Renown* left for Halifax on September 25. A week into the voyage the weather changed and a gale, originating out the south southeast, intensified quickly and pushed up heavy seas.

The storm came on in the morning and continued throughout the day and night. By the next day it reached hurricane force. *Renown* laboured and shook, causing the six men intense anxiety as they figured any minute their vessel would be overwhelmed. Huge seas piled behind the schooner and occasionally one broke across deck. The wind was of such violence that none of the crew could walk against it.

About noon on the second day of the storm, the bowsprit, foremast head, and topsails were carried away. The pounding of the seas against the bulwarks and stern increased the damage to such an extent the schooner began to leak badly. The crew manned the pumps without letup for hours. But despite their labours, the water increased in the hold.

The crew was sure *Renown* would never reach land. Accordingly, they hoisted distress flags to the topmast in case a ship would pass in the distance. For several hours no vessel could be seen. Just as those men had given up hope of coming through alive, a large ship was sighted on the horizon and slowly it turned toward the sinking *Renown*. It was (as they found out later) the steamer S.S. *Glenmay*, bound from Baltimore to Bremerhaven, Germany.

When it drew near *Renown*, the crew of the schooner got out a lifeboat and, after setting fire to their schooner, abandoned ship. In the high winds and waves, it took all their remaining reserves of strength to keep the little craft in line with the steamer. If they had missed it or drifted past, possibly the little boat would have overturned.

On board *Glenmay*, the Newfoundland seamen were treated kindly. In due time the steamer reached its destination where the shipwrecked men were handed over to the British Consul in Germany. They were placed in the Seamen's Home for a few days until arrangements could be made to get them to Germany.

James Courtney, who was suffering from a growth on his forehead, was placed in the hospital. Eventually the shipwrecked crew were transferred to Shields, England, and from there to Liverpool. At Liverpool, they joined the liner *Carthaginian* which brought them to St. John's. On

November 21, 1911, they left by the coastal steamer *Prospero* for their homes in Burgeo.

CATHERINE M. MOULTON ABANDONED, BURGEO

After its cargo of fish was delivered to Spain, the tern schooner *Catherine M. Moulton* loaded salt and sailed for home port Burgeo on October 30, 1926. Built in 1919, at Conquerall Bank, Nova Scotia, the *Catherine M*, as the schooner was commonly called, netted 155 tons and was 119 feet long.

Moulton's business, a long-standing processing and export company in Burgeo, owned the schooner. With the exception of Captain George H. Douglas who belonged to Grand Bank, the crew came from Burgeo and area: mate Henry Standing, bosun Isaac Anderson, cook William Ingraham, sailors George Hann and Edward Janes.

Off the coast of Europe and about six days of sailing to reach Portugal, *Catherine M* met a powerful hurricane head-on. In the battle with the elements, the tern began to leak. It seemed as if the tern and its valiant crew could not avoid the elements as they kept driving in and out of a wind storm for ten days. All hands manned the pumps constantly. They made no headway on leaks as water slowly gained and rose in the hold. Finally the men could work no longer and were simply too exhausted to continue pumping.

By November 18, they had been driven back nearer the coast of Spain and it was then a Spanish sardine steamer saw the beleaguered vessel. The sardine steamer maneuvered alongside and the schooner crew waited for a chance to climb the ropes lowered over the side. The only accident befell William Ingraham who fractured his left leg at the knee during the rescue. *Catherine M. Moulton* sank shortly after.

On Christmas Day 1926, they arrived in Saint John, New Brunswick, on the Canadian Pacific Railway liner *Monclare* and left for Newfoundland the next day.

When the crew of *Catherine M. Moulton* arrived in Saint John, New Brunswick, this is how the front page of December 27, 1925, edition of Moncton's *Daily Times* showed the news. Photo inset of Captain George Douglas. For another story of Captain George Douglas' marine adventures see Chapter 52.

Ascania (above) wrecked near Petites. Shortly after midnight on June 13, 1918, the Cunard Liner *Ascania* went ashore while en route from Liverpool to Montreal. The course of the route would take it south of the south coast of Newfoundland, but through some navigational error and heavy fog, the great steamer struck rocks near Rose Blanche Point located about twenty-five miles east of Cape Ray.

It had a crew of 191 and carried nine passengers; only one was a woman, stewardess Miss Battley. Three passengers were Marconi operators travelling to the Pacific coast. There were two soldiers returning from the World War I European front and one passenger was a priest.

The passengers and several crew rowed into Rose Blanche to report *Ascania*'s forehold full of water. By June 17, eighty crewmen arrived in Port aux Basques and indicated the ship would never be refloated. In fact the hulk was a danger to local navigation.

The captain and fifty crew remained on the stranded liner, awaiting the arrival of a salvage steamer, but by June 18, they had to abandon ship as *Ascania* was breaking up. Final reports said that at high tide it was completely submerged and about four feet showed at low tide. Over the years several artifacts from this ship have been salvaged, including an officer's mahogany desk, oak chairs, a table, and silverware. Photo courtesy of Hubert Hall, SHIPSEARCH Marine, Yarmouth.

Chapter 6

Three Brothers to the Rescue

A t 9 a.m. on March 9, 1974, the herring seiner *Silver King II* left Grand Bank for Harbour Breton. It was under the command of Ephriam MacDonald, age fifty-one and with him were three crew: his two sons Gerald and Ernest Bryan, both in their twenties and engineer George Leamon, sixty-three. All were from Burnt Islands on Newfoundland's south coast.

One hour out of port and fifteen miles from Harbour Breton, the fifty-ton vessel began to leak and although the crew tried to keep water out, they couldn't keep it under control. Captain MacDonald turned back to Grand Bank, nine miles away. Sea water soon covered and stalled the engine, setting *Silver King II* adrift. With no power the captain was unable to radio for help.

Captain MacDonald recalled:

> From ten thirty to two thirty we drifted driven by a thirty-five mile an hour northwest wind. When *Silver King* was a quarter mile off shore we tried to keep it from drifting ashore by dropping anchor.
>
> We decided to abandon ship which was still taking on water. One man got into a rubber life raft and I and two others got into a dory. When the dory was approximately 100 feet off shore, the breaking seas filled it with water and we were thrown into the sea.

Two men, including the one in the rubber raft, managed to reach shore through the breakers; however George Leamon became tangled in a rope tied to one of the life belts and couldn't move. "I was trying," said the captain, "to free him, but I just couldn't manage it. Then before I realized it, three men were running out from the beach through the water."

The seventy-nine-foot *Silver King II*, owned by BC Packers of Harbour Breton, lies a derelict on Little Barachois Beach, six miles from Grand Bank. On the evening of March 9, 1974, the seiner drifted ashore and the bottom was nearly torn out. Photo courtesy Norman Drake.

They were three Savoury brothers from Grand Bank: Clyde, Henry, and Kevin. They held the nearly unconscious engineer up out of the water while MacDonald untangled the rope from around his legs. The three brothers then dragged the two seamen to safety, helped the two already ashore to their car about a mile away, and rushed all four to the Grand Bank hospital.

The young Savoury men had been walking to their summer cabin near Little Barachois when they saw the dory and life raft leave the vessel. By the time they ran the one and half miles to the scene, the skipper and engineer were still in the water. The young men were there in time to rescue and to keep the Burnt Islands fishermen from freezing to death on a bitter day. In December, Newfoundland's Lieutenant-Governor Gordon Winter presented the Savoury men with bravery certificates.

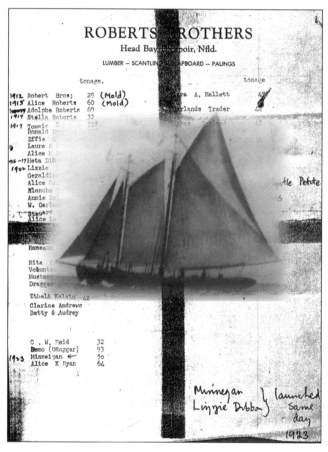

The Roberts Brothers of Baie d'Espoir began building vessels in 1916 and launched thirty-five ships from its yards up to 1935. After that year the building tapered off. The brothers, Morgan and Skipper Wilson Roberts, averaged about two vessels a year and in one year built three. *Tommy G* and *Ronald M. Douglas* were the two tern schooners built there; the latter at 198 tons was the largest. *Shirley Blanche*, 1949, was the last.

Photo inset of Roberts' fifty net ton schooner *Minnegan*, launched on the same day in 1923 as their *Lizzie Dibbon*. *Minnegan* (later renamed *Telic*) was commanded or owned by various individuals: Captain Edward Hillier, Fortune; William Dicks, North Sydney; and James E. Strong of St. John's. It was also the first command of Charles B. Thornhill, Fortune. *Telic* was condemned and pulled on a beach to rot at Little Bay Islands. Images courtesy of Stella Roberts.

Chapter 7

Shipwreck Coast

The papers of the day called the work "yeomen service." When the steamer *Montpelier* piled ashore at Big Yankee Rock near Channel on May 4, 1900, two residents of Port aux Basques, John Musseau and James Anderson, worked diligently to rescue the crew. Captain J.E. Galt and his twenty-nine crew were saved by local men including Musseau and Anderson who went back and forth in their small boats until all were taken off. Filled with ballast, *Montpelier* broke off at the Number One hatch — the bow remained upright on the rock.

For several years after the ship was abandoned certain enterprising fishermen would cut or take square pieces of iron from it. The iron replaced the back of their stoves. Coal burned so hot it damaged the stove and *Montpelier* iron repaired it. Then for many years after that local fishermen prevented anyone from salvaging iron from the *Montpelier* wreck for not only was the "Old Ship" a landmark for local vessels, but it was used as an iron anchor for small fishing craft. On May 1, 1968, the hulk disappeared in a storm.

Montpelier's loss was attributed to a strong southeasterly wind, high waves, and foggy conditions. Over the years however, small islands, sunken reefs, and dangerous ledges claimed many a ship off Port aux Basques and Cape Ray. One of the most dangerous was a ledge called

"The Brandies," a shoal three quarters of a mile off Cape Ray.

This section recounts some memorable accidents around Port aux Basques for a period of about 100 years between 1831-1930.

The 2,248-ton *Montpelier* (above) was owned by the South African Steamship Company and was headed to Quebec from Liverpool, England. According to local stories, it carried Spanish gold. Local men were known to have dug the gold pieces out from cracks in the rock using special tools they devised especially for that purpose. Photo courtesy of Maritime History Archives, Harry Stone Collection.

The wreck of *Montpelier* is one in a long chronology of marine calamities that occurred near the southwest corner of Newfoundland. One of the oldest recorded wrecks near Port aux Basques is that of the passenger ship *Lady Sherbrooke*. It went ashore on July 19, 1831, near Mouse Island under mysterious circumstances which hinted on intentional scuttling. Captain Gambles, a seaman, and twenty-seven passengers survived, but 268 men, women, and children perished.

According to local stories, *Lady Sherbrooke* carried gold. In the 1930s and 40s some residents would dynamite rocks on Mouse Island to get at gold coins in the crevices and as well they made special tools for digging deep into the cracks.

Many of the bodies from *Lady Sherbrooke* were buried in Port aux Basques in a part of town today referred to as Mouse Island. One can still see the mounds of earth with no markers from the mass burials. Many victims, interred hastily because of decomposition and the fear of disease, were buried with everything they were found with — jewellery, money, and other personal effects.

Fifty years later, on May 28, 1878, the topsail schooner *Mary Walter* journeying from Bay of Islands to St. John's with a cargo of herring, hit the Brandies. The day was clear and fine, the sea smooth, leaving most people to wonder how the ship ended up on the rocks. *Mary Walter* had to be beached one and a half miles east of Cape Ray for repairs, but on June 2, it sank in deep water.

On November 12, 1884, the barque *Atlas* sailing from Quebec to Liverpool with a large cargo of squared timber, ran ashore on Brandies reef. It refloated on the next high tide and drove to sea. On November 13, schooners from Port aux Basques took the barque in tow, but with a strong southeast gale coming on, they had to abandon it. *Atlas* drove on shore four miles east of Cape Ray and went to pieces.

The next year on April 18, 1885, fire destroyed the lighthouse at Cape Ray. It had been so instrumental in warning ships of the hazardous coastline and reducing ship losses that the Dominion Government replaced it quickly. On July 1, steamer *Napoleon III* arrived at Port aux Basques with material for a new lighthouse, a work gang of twenty men, and their construction foreman. The new lighthouse began operating on August 10, 1885.

Despite the light, wrecks continued. Eight years later on May 3, 1893, the American fishing schooner *Stranger* ran ashore on the Brandies and, although it stayed afloat, was badly damaged. Eight men from the area went on board pumping until May 6 when it was towed to Sydney by the steamer *Havana*.

The steamer *Arcandia*, travelling from Montreal to Hamburg with general cargo struck Red Rocks Point, four miles north of Cape Ray. The weather on that May 16, 1897, day was described as "dense fog and light southeast wind, sea smooth." The crew jettisoned cargo the same day and from May 17 to May 21, local schooners from Port aux Basques salved cargo. On May 22, the steamer refloated. With the help of the wrecking steamer *Lord Stanley*, it reached Port aux Basques and eventually sailed back to Quebec.

When a fully loaded steamer, the 2500-ton ship *Mare Otis*, grounded at Cape Anguille, on June 26, 1900, the wreck remained nearly intact for a month until a small tug arrived to take "baulk" or squared timber from the steamer's deck. *Mare Otis*, a British cargo liner, was practically new, but its bones remained near Cape Anguille.

Two Port aux Basques men, William Carter and Jacob Davis, were in on the salvage of the barque *Comet*, wrecked near Channel on May 17, 1901. They purchased the hull for $250, the chains and anchor for $42 and also bought the vessel's two boats and sails. Nearly everything from *Comet* was auctioned off to residents of the area, but that was not the end of the story. On May 31, fishermen put in an official complaint that a great deal of debris from the wreck damaged their nets. There is no record of compensation.

The next year the steamer *Morena*, laden with pig iron for Montreal, ran ashore on Brandies reef. The next day the crew threw over 200 tons of cargo, but on May 19, Number One and Number Two holds were full of water and *Morena* became a total loss.

Indeed Port aux Basques entrepreneurs were not adverse to travel as far away as St. Pierre to salvage goods — a distance one way of about 160 miles. Most likely the salvagers followed the coastline, making it a much longer journey.

When John Gillam sailed into Port aux Basques on July 20, 1903, with a load of cheese and butter from S.S.

Monterey, wrecked at St. Pierre, other shipowners saw an opportunity for salvage as well. N. Bragg and William Carter left Port aux Basques on July 22, but Carter returned five days later from the *Monterey* site with no salvage. On July 28, Bragg also returned without any goods.

The Brandies became yet again the site of a shipwreck. On June 27, 1904, the S.S. *Mary Hough* struck the Brandies at 7 p.m. while en route to Bonne Bay. Due to the thick fog in the area, local pilot Coffey, an old employee of the Coastal Company and thoroughly acquainted with the coast, had the duty of guiding the ship safely through.

Bowring Brothers owned *Mary Hough* and used the vessel to carry freight and passengers along Newfoundland's south coast. At the time, the weather was fine and wind moderate. After it went aground, all crew and passengers were carried to the shore; Captain Crossett alone stayed with the vessel.

Mary Hough had run high and dry upon the Brandies and the forehold filled with water. It was feared if any wind came up, the bottom would be torn out. As a result Bowrings engaged the services of the American wrecking tug as soon as the tug was finished with R.M.S. *Hibernian* which was aground at Stormy Point Shoal near Codroy. Under the command of Captain Wallace, *Hibernian* bound from Montreal to Glasgow, had 600 head of cattle aboard. This was a relatively new ship, having been built in 1902 and was over 4,000 gross tons.

Mary Hough had a quarter load of goods and a dozen passengers. Mail officer M. Aylward recovered all mail aboard. When the Wreck Commissioner at Port aux Basques went to the site, he declared the ship a total loss. By August 1, the derelict had completely broken up, washed off The Brandies, and much goods drifted into Grand Bay.

One of the less-documented wrecks happened on June 30, 1930. The French fishing vessel, *Notre Dame du*

Salut (Our Lady of Safety), ran ashore at Mouse Island with no loss of life. The steel-hulled vessel, a four master with twenty-four fishing dories, had been bound for the Gulf of St. Lawrence to fish halibut.

The entire crew was forced to stay at Port aux Basques until another French boat arrived and carried them back to France. Older residents remember this vessel as "a beautiful looking ship." Men with dynamite opened the side of the schooner and several residents recalled the windlass, deck engines and dories resting on a local wharf for a long time.

Chapter 8

The Captain's Ordeal

A schooner was seen slowly coming in through Humber Arm. This of itself was not unusual. The Bay of Islands and Humber Arm on Newfoundland's west coast was a busy port in the era of sail. But watchers on the shore noticed something unusual about the schooner; it looked weather-beaten, damaged, and its sails hung untidily from the gaffs.

When the schooner arrived, they realized it was the *Julia B*, owned by a Mr. Haliburton of Port au Port and captained by William H. Butt. For a vessel of that size, *Julia B* would ordinarily carry four or five seamen, but strangely enough Butt was the only one aboard.

In late September 1906, *Julia B* went on a fish collecting trip to Wood's Island and other ports in the Bay of Islands. The Bay of Islands, located on the west coast of Newfoundland, is a large body of water spanning approximately 137 square miles. It is composed of four main parts: an open bay, dotted with about twelve islands, for which the bay was named, and three large arms which extend from the open water eastward: North Arm, Middle Arm and Humber Arm, into which the Humber River empties. Wood's Island, the largest island in the bay, once had a substantial population, but its small communities are now abandoned. Red Island lies close to it.

Julia B had visited several small ports and the work took a week or so. On Saturday evening October 6, it was off Red Island in the mouth of Bay of Islands. The captain and crew saw the signs of dirty weather and anchored *Julia B* in the lee of the island. Before long the breeze grew full blown into a gale of fierce southwesterly winds.

To save the craft, Captain Butt and his three crew put to sea and lay to under a double reefed foresail. When they were about ten miles from land, a sudden and intense squall of wind threw *Julia B* on its beam ends. As the schooner lay on its side, the lifeboat was smashed to pieces and three crew — Michael Gillam, married and belonging to Channel, and two men from Port au Port, William Harris and William Picco — were swept into the sea and drowned. Captain Butt barely saved himself from going overboard and was helpless to save the other three unfortunate men.

At 5 a.m. Monday morning, Butt got into the hold from the forecastle and managed to jettison some fish so that the craft came back to a near even keel. He then kept *Julia B* before the wind which gradually veered from the northwest.

In order to keep the vessel from going on the rocks near shore, he had to hoist the mainsail. In the storm that raged all Saturday night and Sunday, the mainsail had been ripped away by the wind at the double-reef points.

Since *Julia B* still listed out somewhat, seas were continuously breaking over the schooner. Captain Butt had to take great care to keep himself from being washed overboard. Working cross-handed — doing a job that required two or more people — he tried to raise what was left of the torn and damaged mainsail. It was no easy task. When Butt was interviewed by the Corner Brook newspaper *Western Star* he said it took twenty attempts before he finally hoisted and secured the sail.

When the captain pulled into port, he was exhausted and barely able to stand. He had been without food and water for twenty-four hours.

In September 1933, the schooner *Rose L*, owned by Philip E. Lake of Fortune, fished off Newfoundland's west coast. It had taken a full load, but during one of its stops on the coast, several land based fishermen asked Captain Jacob Piercey if he could take their fish. Perhaps they had no way of getting their cured fish to market and saw the schooner as a way to sell their summer's catch. The captain and the fishermen agreed on a fair price, the fish was stacked on deck, and *Rose L* set sail.

Unidentified schooner breached and listing on its starboard side, although this one is probably beached somewhere in the Twillingate area.

But the extra load proved too much for the old schooner. According to the story of its loss, the vessel broke in two amidships somewhere off McDougall's Gulch on September 27. The fourteen men rowed to land, walked up to the train tracks, and hitched a ride on the next train. It happened to be the west bound freight train heading to Port aux Basques. Constable Pike wired the Department of Marine and Fisheries in St. John's saying

"I provided the crew with boarding house. Please advise what to do next."

In time they were given transportation on the east bound coastal boat which took them to their homes in Fortune.

Chapter 9

Disaster on the Labrador

The "floater" families of Conception Bay fished all summer on the Labrador coast or on the French shore — that part of the northern Newfoundland coast which extended from Cape St. John to Cape Ray on the southwest portion of the island. The fishermen returned home in the fall when the season ended or before ice prevented the movement of the ships.

By August 19, 1912, fishing was poor at Huntingdon, on the coast of Labrador. Two Bay Roberts schooners in the area were *Maritime* and *Energy*, both involved in the summer or floater fishery off Labrador.

Captain Dawe of the schooner *Maritime* decided to take up his traps and move further up the coast to the Turnavick Islands. Before that job was completed a storm of wind on August 22 destroyed much of his gear. The next morning, with one trap still in the water at Huntingdon and eight moored on the back of Independent Island, all *Maritime*'s crew, except the captain went to Huntingdon and took up the trap.

That's when trouble started. On the second trip, Captain Dawe with five other men had work to finish at Huntingdon and they went there and took up some moorings. Since there was still gear left in the water at Independent Island, several other men — William Dawe, William Spencer, Richard Jackson, and Edward and

James Holmes — from *Maritime* got out the trap boat to take in this fishing gear around 3 p.m.

Left on board were Azariah Dawe, James Brown, William Parsons, a young boy, and the lady cook for the crew, Ellen Russell who lived in Country Road, once a community near Bay Roberts. Azariah Dawe, with his suit of oil clothes under his arm, was about to go with the men in the trap boat when the captain told him to stay and help James Brown move some fish in the hold.

Weather threw a nasty turn in the ensuing events. Up to 4 p.m. it was calm, but after that time the wind came up from the south and a heavy sea was running. The five men had not showed up and those remaining on *Maritime* began to worry. James Brown recalled:

> They should have been back to the schooner at seven o'clock. When eight o'clock came and they did not return, we began to get uneasy. At nine o'clock we rowed over to the schooner *Energy* and reported the matter to Captain John Kelly.
>
> Returning to our own schooner, we walked the deck until ten o'clock when I noticed something like four sticks drifting toward the vessel.

By now it was dark and whatever the objects were, they could not be distinctly identified. Two men got in the ship's boat and rowed toward the black shape. They had only rowed about a gunshot when their boat struck what they discovered to be part of the trap boat used by the five men about seven hours earlier. Brown said, "I knew then that some misfortune had befallen our comrades and the only hope was that they may have climbed on some rocks or clung to part of the boat and drifted shorewards."

Not long after Captain Kelly's men from the *Energy* came aboard *Maritime*. Once they heard the news of the smashed trap boat, they in all haste went to land, informed Mr. James Dawe, the captain's brother, who initiated a search.

It was 11 p.m. before James Dawe and eight of his men manned a small boat and rowed for Independent Island where they believed an accident had taken place. But the wind and tide were so strong that they were forced to turn back. On board the *Maritime*, the searchers took some lanterns and torches and walked to Mark's Point where they figured the trap boat had been wrecked.

Their hunch proved correct. They discovered part of the broken boat and oars tossed on the rocks by the sea. The next day, Saturday, August 24, the wind blew a hurricane which prevented any boats from searching for the missing men. They walked back to Mark's Point in daylight, but found nothing but wreckage of the trap boat. Crewman James Brown of *Maritime* remembered:

> The following day, Sunday, was fine but a heavy sea was running. William French, a brother-in-law of the captain, walked out to the point by land and, seeing part of the stern of the boat in the water, returned to the harbour and got a trap boat. He went to the scene.
>
> Attached to the stern of the wreckage was a fishing line, on which was found the body of Edward Holmes. The line was caught in the mooring of Henry Brown's trap, about fifteen or twenty fathoms from the point.

Monday and Tuesday saw no letup in the heavy weather. It was not before Wednesday, August 28, before an all out search began. On September 1, eight days after the men went missing, four young men — George Brown, Arthur Kelly, and two Meshers — went to the Cove and found the body of Richard Jackson on the beach. One week after, the body of James Holmes was discovered in Mark's Cove.

Despite an all out search for William Dawe and William Spencer, no trace of their remains was found. Because of the impending winter ice and freeze-up, the captain of *Maritime* had no choice but leave the Labrador coast on September 16.

It could only be assumed that a heavy sea broke on the trap boat as it was passing Mark's Point Rock near Huntingdon. The boat smashed, killing the men or leaving them to struggle helplessly on small pieces of the boat. At the conclusion of his story James Brown sadly remarked, "Such is the history of events of the awful fatality which cost the lives of five of our best fishermen."

S.S. *Imogene* (above) stranded at Boom Rock off Canso, Nova Scotia, on September 21, 1940. In command was Captain Sidney Hill and his crew of twenty-seven men. En route from Turk's Island laden with salt for Gaspe, Quebec, the steamer struck Boom Rock. Holds one and two filled with water and ten hours later it was abandoned. The crew rowed ashore, but later the seas became so rough that salvage was impossible and *Imogene* became a victim of the sea. The 715-ton ship, named after a character in Shakespeare's play *Cymbeline*, was the last vessel built specifically for sealing and participated in the seal hunt from 1929 to 1940.

Designed to cope with Arctic ice with its "icebreaker stem and a cruiser stern," *Imogene* was easily manoeuvred in heavy ice. Because of these features, the ship was involved in several rescue operations in Newfoundland. It went to the aid of the S.S. *Ranger* in Trepassey Bay and towed the stricken vessel to St. John's. In 1931, near the Horse Islands, it provided food and medical supplies for the survivors of the *Viking* disaster.

In 1933, under Captain Albert Blackwood, *Imogene* landed 55,636 seal pelts, the largest number ever landed in one year. In 1938 the captain was Wes B. Kean. Photo courtesy of Dr. Rowe, Don Mills, ON.

Chapter 10

Wreck of E.M.A. Frampton

The story of survival on a barren coast after a shipwreck is best told in the words of the captain, Ralph Tucker. His schooner, the auxiliary coaster *E.M.A. Frampton*, ran aground at West Bluff, Huntingdon Island, off the Labrador coast on October 30, 1951. This vessel, owned by the Frampton business of St. John's, was named after Edward, Maxwell, and Annie Frampton. It had been built by Edmond Frampton in 1935, at Gin Cove, Trinity Bay.

E.M.A. Frampton, an auxiliary vessel, powered by an engine or sail, if the wind was fair, carried general supplies from St. John's to Goose Bay, Labrador, and headed back to Lewisporte. Tucker had five crew: mate George King of Hillview, Trinity Bay; engineer Ralph Brown, Tack's Beach, Placentia Bay, and later a resident of Lewisporte; William Ivany, Ireland's Eye; cook John Brown, Tack's Beach; and Weldon Stoyles. Three passengers, hitching a ride from the Labrador to St. Anthony Bight, made the trip.

Tucker recalled:

> We were coming south from Goose Bay in company with the *Hazel P. Blackwood* on Monday, October 29, when we ran into a howling blizzard north of Dumpling Island.

It was impossible to see anything so we decided to anchor when we were in vicinity of Huntingdon, to spend the night.

By daylight the wind chopped to the northwest at hurricane force and at sixty to seventy-five miles an hour. It was the strongest wind Captain Tucker had ever experienced. The empty schooner rode the waves like a bobber, and even with the anchor out and all chain, the strain tore the windlass from the deck and the starboard race pipe was wrenched from the bow. Tucker recalled:

> The anchor lost grip and the *Frampton* began to drag, drifting directly in a lee shore. I ordered the crew to slip the anchor and put the engines at full speed to get away from the land. After great difficulty and much anxiety, we managed to get out of danger temporarily.
>
> We endeavoured to head into the gale to get to shelter at Dumpling on the windward shore, but the vessel was too light. We were going full out on the engines but were unable to make any headway and we drifted broadside.

The schooner had no radio set and the captain could not contact any other vessel to report its troubles. When the crew tried to slip, or let go the anchor, the shackles were rusted together and could not be freed. Then someone ran below to get two axes, put one axe on the bottom of the rusty shackle and swung the other axe to cut the bolt. *E.M.A. Frampton* drifted toward land. Tucker reported:

> It was then we headed for West Bluff, which could offer shelter, so we moored the vessel to the land with hawsers. On Tuesday evening, October 30, the *Frampton* began to pound on the rocks underneath the hull. It became apparent that we would have to abandon ship.

Collecting together food, the foresail for shelter, bed sheets and clothes, we got the dories ready to attempt a landing. It was impossible to row to land because of the hurricane wind and heaving seas. We managed by hauling along one of the lines we already had ashore.

It was bitter cold and as soon as we had hauled the dories to safety, we went about setting up the foresail for shelter. We collected boughs for bedding and to build a fire outside our camp. It was impossible to lie down and sleep as it was too cold and we, the nine of us, kept moving around all night to keep ourselves warm.

The next morning we saw that the stern lines of the *Frampton* had parted and the schooner had drifted on the shore. Myself and engineer Brown managed to board the vessel by dory and climbed over the bows. It was breaking up but the spars were still standing.

One of the reasons for boarding was to get the small stove which I had in my cabin and which we planned to put up in the camp on the land. We got the stove and a few other articles and hurriedly got ashore. We were afraid the spars and rigging would come tumbling down around us.

They had a line to the shore with the dory attached and as they got the things they needed, the dory was pulled to shore by the crew waiting. Captain Tucker and his men were now stranded on an island with little shelter in a cold November storm. There would be little chance of being seen and days would pass before a vessel would be sent to search for them. Fortunately help was at hand from two sources.

Hazel P. Blackwood had a ship to shore radio set aboard and informed the coastal steamer *Kyle* of the predicament the *Frampton* was in. Tucker says:

During the day, the *Hazel P. Blackwood*, which had managed to get to Dumpling the day previous — due to its greater engine power which could stem against the wind — steamed out to West Bluff, but the sea was too rough to make an attempt to land. We were glad to know that rescue was at hand as soon as weather conditions improved.

On the second night conditions were more comfortable in our camp but far from what we would have liked. We welcomed a lull in the storm and the sight of the S.S. *Kyle* which had come to our rescue. We launched our dories and rowed out to meet the steamer's lifeboats which had come as near as the shoal water would permit.

By 7:30 p.m. on Thursday, the shipwrecked crew of *E.M.A. Frampton* was safe aboard *Kyle*. Captain Tucker was quick to thank *Kyle*'s Captain Edward Joseph O'Keefe and Captain Jordan Blackwood of the *Hazel P. Blackwood*. Tucker and his men were carried to Lewisporte and from there made their way to their respective homes.

Author's note: Some fifty years after the loss of *E.M.A. Frampton*, I talked with engineer Ralph Brown about the wreck. He recalled the events clearly: the troubles the crew had trying to slip the anchor chain and the eventual breakup of the schooner. "The snow that first night on the island," he remembered, "was pretty deep and piled up over our foresail tent. It was so cold we had to go back out to the wreck to get a stove to keep warm."

When he and the captain boarded the pounding schooner, they couldn't stay long for fear the masts would come out and fall on them. The keel was broken up in the surging seas. Brown, in a gesture of kindness for another person, did have time to go below and get a parcel.

The captain of an American tug moored in Goose Bay had a winter coat for his wife in St. John's and, seeing *E.M.A. Frampton* was going to Newfoundland, gave it to him to deliver to her. When Brown went below deck on the *Frampton* for the last time, he saw the bundled coat and brought it to shore with him. In time, he went to St. John's on the S.S. *Kyle* and passed the parcel, intact, to the lady. Brown recalled, "She said 'Thank you' but had no idea what the coat and I went through on a shipwreck on the Labrador coast."

The Framptons asked engineer Brown to sign on with their vessel *Glenwood*, one of the Splinter fleet and owned by the business in 1951. Instead he decided to work on Lewisporte Wholesalers schooner *Evelyn Evans*.

Chapter 11

Tragedy on Little Sacred Island

Great Northern Peninsula/Little Sacred Island/South River

Hundreds of ships and untold scores of lives were lost in Newfoundland in the salt fishing era. For most losses, events are obscure and details of the wreck, the anguish on families, and the toll of economic setback were not usually written down or otherwise recorded. However, *Nelson*'s story has been preserved through a written, first-hand account of one of the survivors — a survivor who battled an October gale on a wind-swept offshore island with no one around to hear or help. The wreck claimed two lives — the writer's brother and also his shipmate.

In mid-October 1939, a devastating storm swept through the northern reaches of Newfoundland. It was Friday, October 20, 1939, before the first reports came to government officials. From places like Little Bay Islands, Cook's Harbour, and Wesleyville employees of the Lighthouse Division of the Department of Public Works telegraphed St. John's to document extensive damage. A sudden gale, which was the tail end of a hurricane, roared through on Tuesday night and Wednesday morning of October 17 and 18. It ravaged several ships, but the information on the *Nelson* came in last as it was wrecked on an isolated island and the surviving crew reached a town several hours later.

Rosalind B, owned by James Strong Limited of Little Bay Islands, Notre Dame Bay, went ashore at Leading Tickles on Wednesday morning. The schooner, carrying a load of wood and fully insured by the Terra Nova Mutual Insurance Company, broke apart but all crew survived. James Hill at Wesleyville on Newfoundland's Straight Shore wired the Department of Natural Resources to say that a schooner had passed Cabot Island in distress. Most of its sail was gone and what was left was tattered.

Hoffe Brothers business at Cook's Harbour, east of Cape Norman on the Great Northern Peninsula, grew concerned about the safety of *Hazel P. Blackwood*. This schooner had left several hours before the storm broke; but it was later learned the schooner made Catalina safely. Another vessel at Catalina, *Dora P. Lane*, returning from the Labrador, was not so fortunate. It went aground on Tuesday with eleven men, two women aboard and a cargo of 1,200 quintals of fish. No one was injured and insurance on the hull made it possible for owners to refloat and repair the schooner.

The final story out of Bay Roberts was the most tragic. The loss of John B. Smith's schooner *Nelson* was carefully set down by his son, Will Smith. The disaster happened on the night of October 18, and Will's sister, Marion then living in Montreal, heard about it and the loss of two lives on the radio shortly after. Will wrote to Marion on October 31 to explain what happened to him and how a brother lost his life.

The seventy-ton *Nelson*, rebuilt from the keel up at Bay Roberts some years before, was returning from the Labrador fishery in the fall of 1939. In his letter, Will Smith described the events as they unfolded — tragically as it turned out.

The schooner left Punch Bowl near Corbett's Harbour on October 17 at 11:30 a.m. Wind and weather were moderate and the crew figured to make South River, the home port, within days.

With owner John B. Smith were his sons: Will, the old-est, Cecil, age thirty-three, and Clarence. Will's son, Jack about sixteen or seventeen, was part of the crew. Others were Lester Batten, George Warford, and Thomas Bussey. The latter, a cousin, may have been a passenger and all belonged to South River, Conception Bay.

Nelson reached Battle Harbour at 8 p.m. and since weather was settled and winds were favourable, Captain Smith decided to press on. This was normal to do for to delay sailing until daylight could, with a shift in wind, mean a loss of days of sailing time. As Captain Smith viewed it, "The glass (barometer) was steady as was every-one's in the vicinity and it showed no sign of a gale until about 1 a.m. Wednesday."

They pushed on. Clarence Smith and Will had the eight to twelve watch that night and as it approached twelve and the end of their watch, the wind had begun to freshen a little. Captain Smith decided to take in the mainsail and run with the whole foresail.

Although it was snowing a little, they could see the light on the north end of Belle Island North and caught the reflection of the south end and Cape Bauld. At twelve three men came on watch: Will's brother Cecil Smith, George Warford, and Leslie Batten. Will went below for a nap, but didn't take off his rubber clothes in case he was called to help handle the ship. Will wrote:

> It began to blow fresh then and Cecil had the wheel and the binnacle light went out. He called me to fix it and I did. Father said we would have to reef the main-sail. When we met he said to me that we are in for a storm. The glass is gone wild. I stepped back in the cabin and looked at the glass. I knew we were in for wind, but we were well fitted for wind, and with plen-ty of sea room, it didn't daunt us.

Within one hour the wind changed from a moderate breeze to the makings of an all-out gale. But there was plenty of water to navigate safely and the crew had a good ship beneath them. But in a storm at sea, there are many things — things which seem small and insignificant in retrospect — that can go wrong. And on the *Nelson* that night the wind flung a halyard, or rope to raise and hold a sail, and put it somewhere it was not supposed to be. That bit of trouble took some extra time and it marked the beginning of the end:

> Then we (relates Will Smith) took in the foresail and in taking it in, the halyards got around the cross trees and stayed there. Then we double-reefed (tied) the mainsail to lie in the Straits. Before we could get the vessel straightened, it came to the wind and went around the other side. It made the rudder catch back water and this broke the rudder post. I was in the cabin getting a light and heard the crack.
>
> Cecil was at the wheel and I called to him to ask what the noise was. He said he didn't know. Shortly after he called me and said the rudder post was broken.
>
> I knew then we were in for it and we were not far from land. It was a blizzard of northeast wind and driving sleet. We could do nothing for awhile but secure our canvas and before long we sighted land right alongside.

Although they didn't know it at the time, it was Little Sacred Island in Sacred Bay off the extreme end of a peninsula north of St. Anthony. The nearest community was Ship Cove/Cape Onion, strung along the shoreline for about two miles and with families of Adams, Andrews, Anstey, Bessey, Edison, and Decker.

Now the Smith men and the other crew were in a fight for their lives. Two men hoisted the staysail to the jib in hopes *Nelson* would clear the island. But it was too late and it struck on the northeast end of the island as Smith reported:

Nelson struck bowsprit first, put the bowsprit right in
on deck. It came back with the sea and another sea hit
the stern. This drove the schooner in head on again
and ground the head to powder. Can you imagine a
cliff about 200 feet high — straight up, if anything
overhanging. A crow couldn't pitch anywhere with
the sea running about thirty feet up. The water was
like a tub of soap suds and blinding snow before
dawn. Water boiled into the vessel.

Not a nice experience, but nobody flinched. It
drifted away from that island (Little Sacred Island)
and then we saw another island right ahead. Anyhow
we had our motor boat on the starboard side and
couldn't hoist it out.

We decided to get in the boat and when the vessel sank it would float off. That's what we did; cut the
rigging and let the boat float. The *Nelson* sank under
us. Anyhow we drifted clear on another island and we
pitched in the water when the boat struck the breakers.

Everyone jumped and swam. Poor Cecil (Smith)
and Tommy Bussey didn't reach the rock where we
landed. Father held on to the boat and it drifted in and
he was saved. Jack (Will's son) was with us and he
jumped and paddled and swam ashore. Then it looked
hopeless.

Hopeless, indeed. On a rock off an island and no sign
of human habitation. It was breaking daylight, but a raging blizzard blew in low temperatures. Everyone was wet.
Two men were gone — the writer's brother Cecil and
Thomas Bussey. If the survivors had the boat which was
probably damaged when it drifted in, they probably had
no oars. Cold and exhausted they had little strength to get
off the crag of rock to the mainland.

To their surprise, people had seen their distress and
reached the island. Although Will doesn't identify them in
his story, they were probably from Ship Cove/Cape Onion.
One man may have been Heber Elliott (originally from

Raleigh) and his sons or brothers and Ches Bessey and Charles Bessey. George Decker may have witnessed the rescue. Smith says:

> Everyone was wet. It was snowing and blowing. In the evening they saw us from the land and came out at the risk of their lives and took us to their houses. They saved our lives.
>
> I don't think we would have lived that night. The wind veered and it froze that night. We were well treated, but with two gone, we didn't feel too good. We couldn't make any preparations (to get off the schooner); everything came too quickly and if you were saved, well. . .
>
> It came near to being a mystery of the sea. We all came within a fraction of death and now we are home destitute for we saved nothing. No insurance except on the vessel.

Will went on to say that he and his son, Jack, "hardly had on a stitch of clothes." All of the other young men found themselves in dire need financially, but they were single with no one depending on them. Will Smith told his sister, it was the same as if he had been dropped from the moon — no cap, shoes, bedclothes, nothing saved whatsoever and not a cent to replace what was lost. The Department of Customs cared for the stranded men and arranged for their transportation back to South River.

Will's father was doing as well as could be expected under the circumstances, but what was most distressing was that up to October 31 the two bodies had not been found.

Chapter 12

So Near, Yet So Far Away

By mid-October the fall fishery on the Labrador coast ended and, usually about two weeks after that, operations wound down on the French Shore. The fishing towns of Croque, Conche, St. Julien's or the Grois Islands were much-frequented harbours in the French Shore fishery. By November though, the schooners had already left for home ports since ice in the northern harbours made movement by sea difficult or impossible.

On Thursday, November 4, 1915, the schooner *Blanche M. Rose* left Grois Islands for St. John's. It had quite a cargo: 1,100 quintals of dry fish below, thirty-six casks of cod liver oil and twenty barrels of herring on deck, plus a motor engine valued at 300 dollars. Nineteen people were aboard — ten men, six women, and three children. The women and children were returning home after a summer living and fishing on Grois Islands.

The forty-five-ton *Blanche M. Rose*, built as a banking schooner at Little Bay in 1900 for Captain John J. Rose of Harbour Breton, was sold to James Baird of St. John's and eventually to Captain William Clemens and his brothers of St. John's. On its final voyage in 1915, most of the crew and passengers were from St. John's. The four Clemens brothers lived on York Street in the east end of the city, but they had fished out of Grois Islands for many years. They had already lost one schooner there; in 1910 their schooner *Highflyer* was wrecked on the islands.

Blanche M. Rose first stopped at Seldom, Notre Dame Bay; then Shambler's Cove in Bonavista Bay. Heavy winds and seas forced Clemens to remain at Shambler's Cove for seven days. When it left on Sunday, November 14, winds were high, forcing the ship to stop at Catalina before proceeding across Trinity Bay to Baccalieu. From Baccalieu Light, Clemens shaped his course for Cape St. Francis.

By this time seas were heavy and the barometer was falling. Clemens decided to run for Carbonear. A sudden squall of wind carried away the foresail and jib. A little later the crew decided to lower the mainsail for that too would have been torn to shreds.

Captain Clemens subsequently anchored to the leeward of Western Bay Point. When both anchors were put out, the crew ran signals of distress up the rigging to attract the attention of the light keeper. Those on *Blanche M. Rose* figured they were about 200 yards from the shore and it would be an easy task for a person on shore to send off a buoy with a line attached. The beleaguered ship and weary crew were tantalizing close to the light, to land, and safety, but there was no response to the signals.

Two crew launched a lifeboat and made an unsuccessful attempt to get to shore and attach a line. From the boat they could see a man moving about near the lighthouse, but all efforts to attract his attention failed. If only a line had been secured on shore, the safety of all aboard, especially the women and children, would have been assured.

It was not to be. The strain on the hawsers from the heavy cross sea running in from Western Bay Point caused the hawsers to burst and at 6 p.m. Tuesday *Blanche M. Rose* was driven to sea. Through considerable effort the crew raised the riding sail and jumbo and the schooner headed for Cape St. Francis. By daylight it was within three miles of Cape Spear and close to St. John's.

Captain Clemens signalled for the St. John's harbour tug. Again the signals were not seen or ignored. Again all aboard were so close to the safety of a harbour; near enough they could see a tug come out and tow a tern schooner into the Narrows.

In the meantime *Blanche M. Rose* was not doing well. As it ran southward under riding sail and jumbo, the schooner was near unmanageable. On Thursday night the crew sighted Cape Race and, although Clemens tried to hold the schooner near land, it was driven to sea.

At daylight Saturday, November 13, the crew saw a large passenger steamer west bound on the horizon. Quickly they ran a flare torch up to the masthead to inform the steamer of distress. Evidently, perhaps because *Blanche M. Rose* had no riding lights, the flare was confused for a guiding light or a position indicator.

Meanwhile relatives and loved ones grew concerned for the safety and whereabouts of the schooner. The last time it had been seen was off Western Bay. There were no communication systems aboard the schooner and it had not reported to any passing ship. *Blanche M. Rose* had seemingly disappeared with crew. On Saturday the harbour tug *D.P. Ingraham* and government tug *Cabot*, commanded by Jacob Kean, were sent to search the seas off Newfoundland's east coast. South southeast of Cape Race, *Cabot* picked up an oil cask. When this was brought back to St. John's a relative of the Clemens' family identified it as from *Blanche M. Rose*. This evidence intensified the anxieties of those waiting for *Blanche M. Rose*'s arrival in St. John's.

Unknown to them, the schooner was in unfamiliar seas as it ploughed through a full-fledged gale off Cape Race. It had lost all sail, anchors and other gear which had been lashed on deck. The pounding of the seas opened seams and it began to leak. For four days only hard work at the pumps kept the schooner afloat.

To make matters worse the vital necessities of life — food, water, fuel — ran short. Enough provisions had been put aboard to last a week from the French Shore to St. John's. Already ten days had passed. For several days a few crumbs of biscuit and some prunes were the only food for the men, women, and children. The package of prunes was on board through a mistake as it had been put aboard at Grois Islands to be returned to another owner and the transfer had not been made.

On Friday, when the prospects of keeping *Blanche M. Rose* afloat any longer were gone, another schooner appeared on the horizon. Quickly distress flags were hoisted in the rigging. As they discovered when the vessel drew near, it was the Newfoundland barquentine *Mary M. Duff* from Carbonear headed for North Sydney for coal.

With careful manoeuvring, Captain George James edged *Mary Duff* near and then put the lifeboat out in charge of bosun Reuben Cole. After several trips, the women and children were transferred to the *Mary Duff*. Seas were so high, each person had to be hauled up over the side of the rescue schooner by a rope around the waist.

When the women and children were safely aboard, *Mary Duff* bore down near the sinking schooner; the crew of the latter jumped aboard *Mary Duff* when the two vessels hit together. In the collision the rails and stanchions of the disabled vessel were smashed and it is thought *Blanche M. Rose* must have sunk not long after it was abandoned.

Although the schooner was insured, the cargo, valued at 10,000 dollars, was not and it represented the potential earnings of the crew. The loss meant a harsh winter for the families. *Mary M. Duff* continued its trip to North Sydney landing the six women, three children and ten men to that port. They were taken to Central House where the owner, Patrick Grant, cared for them until they secured transportation to Newfoundland. The first news of the fate of the nineteen people came with this message to Robert Duff at Carbonear who relayed it to Minister of Marine and Fisheries Archibald Piccott:

> Schooner *Mary Duff* arrived at North Sydney with
> nineteen people taken off the schr. *Blanche M. Rose*;
> instruct C.& W. Hackett, Sydney, re forwarding des-
> tination.

Piccott made arrangements to have them brought
home via *Mary M. Duff*. Those rescued were William
Clemens (which St. John's newspaper mis-spell as
Clements); his brothers Joseph and Michael; William's
adopted son Thomas, age thirteen; brothers Patrick and
Anthony Gardiner; Bernard Gardiner, son of Patrick;
James Penney of Catalina; Nicholas Furlong; Robert
Foley; Mrs. Ellen Tobin and her three children, Albert, age
eight, Julia, age four and John, a baby only thirteen
months old; Mary Locke; Annie Foley; Lucy Foley; Alice
Duke and Annie Barnes. The last two worked for
Clemens' business, while the other women and children
were passengers.

This was not the end of the matter for in early
December an accusation of irresponsible behaviour surfaced in the newspaper *Mail and Advocate*. The newspaper editors asked the Minister of Marine and Fisheries to
check into the conduct of the lighthouse keepers at
Western Point saying:

> If the keeper Edmund Butt had thrown a small rope
> attached to a piece of wood into the sea, the wind
> would have swept it toward the schooner. It would
> have been caught by the *Blanche M. Rose*'s crew and
> used to haul ashore the schooner's big line which
> would have ensured the safety of the vessel and crew.
> The schooner was no further than fifty fathoms from
> the shore.

The article contended that if the light keeper had
responded he would have prevented the loss of $8,000
worth of cargo and avoided the mental and physical tor-
ture the nineteen people went through. It is not known if

any investigation was ever conducted or if it was just a case of the light keeper or his helper not seeing the troubled *Blanche M. Rose* when it was so close to safety yet so far away.

HMS *Calypso*, rigged first as a three-masted barque, in its glory days. It came to Newfoundland about 1900 and shortly after became a training and drill ship for the newly formed Royal Newfoundland Naval Reserve. During the Great War, over 1,500 Calypso-trained (re-named *Briton*) sailors saw action all over the world.

In the 1930s-50s, it was used for salt and coal storage in St. John's harbour. It then was moved to Lewisporte to serve again as a salt-storage hulk. As a rusty and ravaged derelict in a cove north of Lewisporte and near Embree, it died a lonely life for such a proud ship.

Chapter 13

Irene May Explodes off Lewisporte

Musgrave Harbour/Carmanville/Lewisporte

n the 1950s, coasting vessels carried freight and general supplies to the smaller towns and isolated settlements of Newfoundland and Labrador. These ships were generally not converted bankers or fishing ships, but were often built specifically to carry freight and were called freighters or coasters.

Owners had a general business plan: find a load of goods — flour, food, coal, oil, salt fish, lumber or any material that could be carried on deck or below — and deliver it around the coast. To make a profit and to keep their business viable, small vessel operators had no choice but to sail, often overloaded, in adverse weather.

Nor were they particular about the type of cargo, anything and everything to make up a paying load. In the era of the coasters, the large government passenger steamers were not permitted for safety purposes to take dangerous goods, i.e. gasoline and oil. This freight was carried by smaller motor vessels which also had the advantage of maneuverability in a confined harbour and the narrow passages between the islands.

This is the story of the end of the M.V. *Irene May*, a wooden coaster with an engine, as the title MV implies. At one period of its long career, it was owned and skippered by Mark Sheppard of St. John's.

Stewart Abbott, a seaman from Musgrave Harbour, joined the M.V. *Irene May* at Carmanville on the first day of spring 1952, and he remembers its final hours. Captain Elim Parsons of Carmanville operated the eighty-one-ton schooner. That spring Parsons had with him his brother Melvin, the engineer, and three deck hands from Musgrave Harbour, Lod Abbott; and brothers Jasper and Stewart Abbott.

Irene May, Abbott recalled, had two engines, a diesel Kelvin and a semi-diesel engine. The vessel first went to St. John's for freight and general supplies slated for towns located along the northeast coast and Notre Dame Bay. In May, it steamed to Sop's Arm in White Bay for lumber. Abbott remembered:

> In late May, Captain Parsons learned there was a freight of oil in drums to be delivered from Lewisporte, Notre Dame Bay, to Morton's Harbour on New World Island. There was around 1,000 drums of oil and we worked like dogs getting it loaded on deck and below.
>
> We left Lewisporte in the evening of June 6. Ordinarily we could have gone down the inside run, but we were well-laden and we went out around. I was just gone down off the watch and the skipper had the wheel on the next watch.
>
> Then someone shouted, "Fire!" and before I had chance to get on deck the skipper came right out of the wheelhouse out on deck, from the force of the explosion. It took part of the after deck right clean out of the vessel. Now the fire was going below.
>
> What happened see was that there was an oil drum in the gangway to the engine room and gasoline to start the engine ran down through in that one. The gas from a drum meant fumes and gas and the leaks caught. Whew, away it goes and we came on deck, all hands.

With no time to save clothes or personal effects, the crew hastily launched the dory. The engines were still running and this must have made the escape from the dory dangerous. There was no time to lose. Fear of a massive explosion from the cargo of oil was uppermost on the minds of the crew. Abbott says:

> There wasn't much we could do only take the dory and put it out over the side. When we threw it over, it came upright and we jumped in it, just like we were. We rowed away with whatever strength we could. When we were far enough away, the skipper turned the boat so he could see it and tears came to his eyes when he saw his vessel in flames.
>
> *Irene May* was drifting down now; the engines had cut off. We followed and watched it in the dory until it burned through. By and by the main gas off the Kelvin engine caught and out poured the smoke, the black smoke. With the deck burned through, the foremast and mainmast fell, the anchors and chains fell off the bow. The two spars went ahead like that, over the head.

Eventually *Irene May* grounded near Sceviour's Island, several miles northeast of Lewisporte. The inside, deck, and bulwarks were ablaze. The five crew stood far enough off to keep out of any danger of explosion, but close enough to watch the final hours of the schooner.

> The railway steamer *Northern Ranger* was coming in to Lewisporte from Notre Dame Bay. We waved and did everything we could for we thought it could see the fire and smoke, but the steamer never altered course nor slowed down.
>
> We had those steel drums aboard with the big stoppers on them. In the heat of the fire the heads came out of the drums; they just blew out. All them old drums were all blown to pieces and the ones with

the steel stoppers would go up in the air just like you would squirt water.

When the explosions were over and *Irene May* stopped near this island, we knew to try to get a line aboard. We couldn't leave it down in the ship's run and we didn't want it to go in on the island either. If we could get the dory grapnel in over the taffrail to pull the schooner back, it wouldn't beach on the rocks.

I was in the head of the dory and took the grapnel in my hands to chuck it in over the rail. When I got near, I reached up and looked down. The two engines were just like a piece of smoke, like rusted junk. Only a couple of hours before they were worth looking at, now they were all burned out.

The skipper took the ax and chopped the *Irene May* outside on the waterline and once the water started to go in, the wreck had to go down.

It happened there was a boat coming out from Lewisporte, a passenger boat, and it came near us after our vessel sank. We got into Lewisporte and had no personal possessions or extra clothes and there was no one to give us a shirt. We had nothing.

Chapter 14

Danger in the Lumber Trade

Campbellton/Catalina/Port Union

Nancy *Lee* had a short life in the foreign trade. Five years after its launch the schooner was abandoned in the Atlantic. Captain John J. Wiltshire of Catalina/Port Union was in command with his crew: bosun Thomas Walters, P. Boutcher, J. Eastman, N. Banfield, and L. Snowdon. Unfortunately only the last name and no place of residence has been recorded for the crew. When they arrived in St. John's on November 13, 1925, aboard the S.S. *Sachem* the captain and crew were in good health, but they had experienced an ordeal they did not want to repeat very quickly.

Nancy Lee was built to carry wood products from Campbellton to St. John's and New York. But in the end the proud schooner sank, carrying fish from Labrador to Spain.

In 1911, the Horwood Lumber Company of St. John's, which had acquired rights to cut timber near Campbellton, Notre Dame Bay, began construction of a steam-operated lumber mill at nearby Garden Cove and decided to add a pulp mill to their saw mill operations at Campbellton. In 1914, the mill began producing pulp. One year later the main dam failed and power couldn't be produced. When the dam broke again the next year, the mill closed. Only one shipment of pulp was made.

From the early 1900s, lumbering became the exclusive employment in Campbellton and the resulting boom drew people in from all parts of Notre Dame Bay and White Bay including families of Anstey, Bennett, Bert, Brett, Brown, Budger, Callahan, Chippett, Clancy, Clark, Curtis, Evans, Hillier, Hodder, King, Luff, Lushcombe, Perrip, Rowsell, Snelgrove, Snow, Wells, and Young. From 1901 to 1921 the lumber industry drew nearly 300 people to the community; many found full employment harvesting logs.

In the years of the lumber trade, the Horwood carpenters built the 114-ton tern schooner *Nancy Lee* near Campbellton. Built and launched in 1920, it had an overall length of 116 feet.

According to Calvin Evans in his book *For the Love of a Woman*, in which he describes shipbuilding in Northern Arm and in Notre Dame Bay, "Robert Evans of Northern Arm began the building of *Nancy Lee* and Sam Simmons of Campbellton finished the job . . . and Alexander Locke was part of the team." On one of its first voyages, Simmons went as captain to deliver a cargo of pulp from the Campbellton mill to New York.

There was not enough work for a large tern schooner delivering only wood products and toward the end of its career carried fish. *Nancy Lee* left Smokey and Emily Island, Labrador, during the first week of October in 1925, with 275 tons of salt fish, bound to Spain. The voyage started well enough; there was a pleasant breeze, but the hope of a reasonably worry-free trip was soon dashed.

Nancy Lee ran into the terrible weather that prevailed all over the North Atlantic. Captain John Wiltshire described it as "a living west-north-west gale." He and his men could make no headway. They could barely get on deck to shorten sail.

For twenty days the schooner was tossed about; its deck swept from stem to stern and everything moveable washed overboard. Worse than all that, it sprang a leak and the crew took to the pumps. Whenever they got a chance to look up or pause from unremitting labours, nothing could be seen but mountains of water pounding down on *Nancy Lee*. Rails, bulwarks, and stanchions were swept away. Water poured into the galley and cabin and the crew found it nearly impossible to cook food.

It was apparent the schooner would soon founder and, clinging to their last hope, the crew pumped frantically although they were exhausted beyond words. After doing all they could to keep the ship afloat, the captain decided it was no use. They had to abandon the vessel. At 10 p.m. on October 23, the S.S. *Benvorlich* hove in sight and, in response to signals from *Nancy Lee*, slowly turned toward the beleaguered schooner.

In such weather it was impossible to lower a boat, but the steamer stood by until daylight. Its crew waited and watched all night, ready to risk all should the wallowing schooner sink.

In the morning the work of transferring the men began. It was no easy job; whitecaps broke around them and a strong wind hampered work. *Benvorlich* steamed up to the windward and lowered a lifeboat. *Nancy Lee*'s crew clambered aboard. The steamer then went to the leeward, thus enabling the small boat to be driven by the wind in the direction of the wallowing schooner.

Eventually the transfer was accomplished and *Benvorlich* continued its journey to Dublin, Ireland. Before Wiltshire left his schooner he set it afire to prevent the abandoned derelict from becoming a hazard on the Atlantic.

The shipwrecked mariners were landed at Dublin and then transferred to Liverpool, England. There the Mariners' Society supplied them with new clothing and housed them at the Sailor's Home. In November, they joined the S.S. *Sachem* bound for Newfoundland.

One of the most devastating sea tragedies to hit the Horwood Lumber Company was the disappearance of schooner *Percy Wells*. Built in Hare Bay in 1919, especially designed to carry wood, the schooner left Campbellton for New York with a cargo of Horwood

Lumber Company products. On September 25, 1921, it loaded coal for the steam engines at the lumber mills and left New York. En route, *Percy Wells* probably met a treacherous Atlantic storm. No one really knows. The ship and crew — Captain F. Hanham, Luke Feltham, Charles Brown, Peter Noftall, A. Snow of Spaniard's Bay, and Solomon French of Bay Roberts, married with a family — disappeared somewhere en route.

When shipwright Samuel Simmons' sons house was taken down, this photo of tern schooner *Nancy Lee* was located. Although the photo is not sharp, it is believed to be the only image of *Nancy Lee*. The ship has a load of lumber on the foredeck, while a large skiff lies on deck between the masts. It is known that Wesley Collins was a crew member at one point when the schooner went to Sydney for coal. Photo courtesy of Emma (Simmons) Currie, Clarenville, formerly of Campbellton.

On the day *Nancy Lee*'s crew arrived, news came to St. John's that a Carbonear schooner *Toreda Jane*, owned by E.T. Taylor, had gone down. On November 11, 1925, *Toreda Jane*, loaded with 300 quintals of salt cod and barrels of cod oil on deck, began to leak off the Bonavista Peninsula and went down off Melrose. Captain

E. Smith, who belonged to Butter Cove, Trinity Bay, and his crew rowed into Catalina.

THE EVENING TELEGRAM, ST. JOHN'S, NEWFOUNDL. NOVEMBER 13, 1925—6

Loss of Schooner "Nancy Lee"

Captain and Crew Return by Sachem.

This how the November 13, 1925, edition of the *Evening Telegram* described the loss of *Nancy Lee* when the crew arrived in St. John's.

Chapter 15

The Ophir on Penguin Islands

Penguin Islands/Little Bay Islands

In early October 1909, the crew of schooner *Ophir* had a narrow escape from death on the Penguin Islands. *Ophir*, a forty-seven-ton schooner owned and operated by Captain Thistle of Little Bay Islands and laden with winter provisions, left St. John's for Little Bay Islands.

On the journey, *Ophir* had to pass the Penguin Islands off Newfoundland's Northeast Coast or Straight Shore. Extending out from the east point of South Penguin Island, is a series of underwater ledges separated by deeper water. In calm weather small fishing boats can pass through, but in a storm, such as the one Captain Thistle faced about 8 p.m. on October 5, it was a treacherous passage.

The crew double reefed the foresail and for a few minutes *Ophir* ran before the wind. Before the crew finished, the schooner struck the rocks off South Penguin. For three hours they huddled in the rigging, looking for a place to land if and when they got a chance to launch the small lifeboat. They knew it would be madness and suicide to even attempt to hold the lifeboat by the side of the schooner.

During the three hours, Captain Thistle had more than wreck and weather to worry about. After the ordeal was over, Thistle said one of the crew "lost his reason" and wanted to get the boat out immediately. When refused he lost his senses and had to be restrained. Thistle ordered the lifeboat raised above the deck in the "burtons" so the seas would not break it up.

When the moon came out, Thistle saw that he was on the reef off the South Penguin and decided to use the boat to reach the island. After a desperate struggle they reached the rocky shoreline; one of the men who jumped first to a rock was knocked off by a wave, but the next sea swept him back on. All were drenched to the skin on a cold night.

A cask of kerosene drifted on the beach which the marooned crew broke open. One man had a few dry matches in a tin box; soon they had a good fire going supplied with debris from the wrecked *Ophir*. They partially dried their clothing and warmed themselves until daylight. The man who had become disoriented and mad with fear gradually regained his senses and, by daylight, had calmed down.

The fire attracted the attention of others. The light keeper on North Penguin Island, Esau Gillingham, saw the fire, but could not get to the island because of the weather. At daybreak he launched his dory and with a wide detour to avoid the line of underwater reefs, somehow maneuvered his dory offshore from the stranded seamen. With a rope he pulled the crew to safety and carried them to the warm confines of the North Penguin lighthouse.

Esau Gillingham, born in Ochre Pit Cove, Conception Bay, was the first keeper of the Penguin Island light — erected in 1890 — a position he held until 1916. In later years Esau Gillingham was awarded the Imperial Service Medal by King George V for his bravery and service. It was presented by Magistrate Cook of Fogo before a large gathering in the Wesley Hall in Musgrave Harbour.

Several hours after the wreck of *Ophir*, people at Musgrave Harbour people could see, with the aid of a telescope, figures of men on the desolate South Penguin. Wind and wave prevented rescuers from getting out to the island. The news of a wreck was relayed to St. John's and to Jesse Whiteway, a Member of the House of Assembly and who was born in Musgrave Harbour.

When Whiteway learned of the wreck he went to the Minister of Marine and Fisheries, Archibald Piccott. Piccott also had a message from Fogo concerning the wreck and he arranged for the S.S. *Louise* to proceed to the Penguin Islands to take the men off. Later *Ophir*'s shipwrecked crew travelled to their homes at Little Bay Islands by the S.S. *Prospero*.

During the same storm of October 5-6, another schooner, owned by Captain J. Newman of Boyd's Cove, was wrecked at the entrance to Joe Batt's Arm, Fogo Island. The crew had a narrow escape from drowning, but the ship, its load of fish, and thirty barrels of salt all went to the bottom.

Penguin Islands was the scene of another wreck on November 28, 1926, when *Union Jack* (above) struck rocks on north east point of North Penguin Island. Built in Monroe, Trinity Bay, in 1918 by Emanuel Stone, the tern was 121 feet long. In command of Captain Martin Frampton, *Union Jack* left Seldom with a cargo of lumber and logs. Lighthouse keeper Steven Gushue saw the wreck, lit a fire to guide the lifeboat in, and cared for the shipwrecked sailors until the S.S. *Susu* came to pick them up. Photo courtesy of Maritime History Archives.

In 1935, *R.M. Symonds*, a banking schooner built in Bridgewater, Nova Scotia, met its end near the Penguins.

In 1930 its registry changed from Nova Scotia to Newfoundland and the new owner was John F. Parrott of St. Bernard's, Fortune Bay. Not long after it was registered anew to an owner in Bonavista Bay and underwent extensive repairs, alterations and had an engine installed.

R.M. Symonds' crew list for various years has been recorded. In 1932 its crew was mostly from Bonavista Bay: Captain Richard Easton, age thirty-one; cook Eli Feltham, twenty-four, both of Deer Island; mate Kenneth Feltham, forty-two; seamen Samuel Feltham, of Bragg's Island; Raymond Granter, twenty-one, Greenspond; R.A. Newman, Petites; Mark Roberts and Herbert Roberts of Wesleyville. In 1935 the crew was listed as Captain Wilson Holmes, thirty-five; Fred Holmes, twenty-seven, both of Seldom; mate Charlie Kelloway, twenty-three, Wesleyville; cook H. Parrott, thirty-three, St. John's; and engineer William White, twenty-seven, St. Phillips. Captain Mark Roberts was at the helm when the schooner was lost near the Penguin Islands on September 10, 1935.

Chapter 16

Praise Be to the Lightkeeper

Harry's Harbour/Silverdale/Penguin Island/Musgrave Harbour

Our ancestors who lived in Notre Dame Bay, Green Bay and the along the Baie Verte Peninsula didn't have it easy when the time came to secure sugar, flour, salt, and other provisions for the long cold winter. Generally they were self-sufficient people: growing their own vegetables, curing fish and sawing lumber, but for the basics — salt, sugar, flour — they depended on schooners sailing to and from St. John's. Up to the 1960s, there was no trans-island highway and shipping freight by train was not feasible. Branch lines didn't reach many areas.

Their highway was the sea lanes between the northern Newfoundland coasts and St. John's. After the Labrador and inshore fishery ended in October or November and before the ice set in, ship owners and merchants sent their sailing vessels east for supplies. The fall winds and December storms played havoc on men and ships; many were lost en route.

Generally the voyages were made in short passages or "legs." A trip in fair winds from St. John's to Little Bay Islands or Green Bay, for example, lasted between one to two weeks. The first stop was Catalina where crews would rest. The next morning they sailed to Seldom on Fogo Island. The third leg was from Seldom to Herring Neck and Twillingate and then the final sail to home — if everything went well.

Not all stories of hardship, wreck, and ruin have been recorded, but there is a brief description — actually a letter of praise — written by a seaman of Harry's Harbour. A fishing and lumbering community, Harry's Harbour is located northwest of Springdale and straddles two large bays. People on the south side are in Notre Dame Bay while those living on the north side are in Green Bay. Harry's Harbour first appears in the Newfoundland *Census* of 1874 with a population of forty-six, predominately Methodist. According to local tradition, the pioneers were Jeremiah Upward from Bournemouth, Dorsetshire, England, and James White, from Hanly, also in Dorsetshire. They were followed by Kings, Englands, Doreys, Evans, and Verges.

In 1926 a descendant of Jeremiah Upward, Robert Upward (Jr.), was a sailor on the *Fanny W. Freeman*. Under the command of J. Wallace Batstone of Silverdale, the sailing schooner *Fanny W. Freeman* left St. John's on Monday, August 18, 1926. It had a load of supplies and machinery for Hampton, White Bay, where the International Paper Company had a logging operation. Built in Gloucester in 1912, the *Freeman*, as the vessel was often called, was eighty-seven-feet long, twenty-three-feet wide and netted ninety-one tons.

On the following Wednesday night, August 20, the *Freeman* was off the Northeast Coast — the Straight Shore, an area noted for many shipwrecks. While under full sail the vessel struck the rocks off the Penguin Islands. The foremast broke and fell following the impact. As a result, the ship and crew were stranded twenty or thirty feet from shore. The only explanation for the accident was that a strong tide carried the schooner off course and too close to treacherous reefs. The crew survived, but only because of the heroic efforts of the Penguin Island light keeper who rigged a bosun's chair to get them off the wreck.

The bravery and kindness shown by the lighthouse keeper prompted Robert "Uncle Bob" Upward to write about the ordeal and how a light keeper on a remote island saved his life and the lives of his shipmates. Although the shipwreck happened in August, it was late November before Upward sat down to pen a letter to the Newfoundland Superintendent of Lighthouses, William Patterson Rogerson in St. John's.

The lighthouse at North Penguin Island. Photo courtesy of the late Ray Guy.

The letter to Rogerson praised the efforts of Arthur Goodyear and his wife, saying:

> When the lightkeeper and his wife heard our calls for assistance, they lost no time coming to our rescue. They then made a fire out of some oil and hay so they could see our position. On board we had nothing to help ourselves; our boat was smashed and the deck was awash.
>
> The keeper, by means of a rope around his waist which was held by his wife, was able to approach (by wading into deeper water in his sock feet to prevent slipping) nearer than he otherwise could have. He was able to throw a jigger aboard and by this means we were able to make fast a line from our schooner to the shore and we were quickly pulled ashore.

Upward went on to describe how kind and helpful the Goodyears were in the four days he and the crew of *Fanny W. Freeman* spent on the island while awaiting favourable weather to leave. The men had saved no belongings only the clothes they stood in. The sailor who had just finished his watch had turned in bunk for the night and was dressed only in his underwear. The rescuers found clothing for all. Goodyear, a veteran of World War I and a resident of Musgrave Harbour, was married to a war bride, Janette (Neta), a Scottish lady and had two children, Malcolm and Jean.

By the next morning in the heavy sea that pounded the coastline, there was little left of the vessel to be seen. *Fanny Freeman's* cargo was valuable for the wood gathering enterprise at Hampton and consequently the steamer *Earl of Devon* was sent to Penguin Island to salvage it. In the high seas that was impossible. Both schooner and cargo were claimed by the waters off North Penguin Island.

By the 1960s, sailing ships were all but obsolete in towns like Harry's Harbour, Little Bay Islands, Pilley's Island, and Triton. Many Labrador schooners had been converted to motorized coasters, but even their days were numbered. With the completion of the Trans Canada Highway across Newfoundland in 1965 and with improvements to branch roads leading out to White Bay, Green Bay, and Hall's Bay, the trucking industry supplanted the coasting schooner.

In the early 1930s, Captain Wallace Batstone built the eighty-ton *Norman M. Batstone* to replace the *Fanny* and this schooner lasted until June 21, 1957, when it ran ashore at Melrose. As for "Uncle Bob" Upward, he lived a full and rich life in Harry's Harbour where some of his descendants reside today.

Chapter 17

Two Stories from the Straight Shore

Brookfield/Wesleyville/Newtown

In May 1916, the schooner *Reciprocity* left Brookfield, Bonavista Bay, headed for St. John's to obtain supplies for the summer fishery. Owned by Captain Jacob Kean of Wesleyville, *Reciprocity* was commanded by Captain Peter Blackmore. With him were seamen Aubrey Howell, Levi Gill, Albert Dowding, Malcolm Lane, Aaron Rogers, and Garland Gill. The vessel netted sixty-eight tons and had been built in 1903.

During the voyage, *Reciprocity* sailed with fair winds and full sails from Bonavista Bay to St. John's, and by the early morning of May 20, it had reached the waters off the Narrows. At 8:00 a.m. and while off St. John's, Captain Blackmore waited to see if a harbour tug would tow them into port. Normally ships like *Reciprocity*, if winds and seas were favourable, could navigate the narrow passage without difficulty. But that day a high wind blew offshore, seas were high, and it would be best to get towed through the Narrows.

The crew had hoisted the signal flag, indicating a tug was required, when a squall of wind hit the schooner. Before the crew could attend to the sails and sail the vessel from the land, it struck the cliff at Wash Balls near Freshwater. *Reciprocity* stayed on the ledge, pounding in the rock and surf. The crew feared it would smash to pieces in no time.

They launched the lifeboat and in doing so, the fall (the hoisting tackle rope) gave out and the crew launched the boat manually. In the arduous task of getting the little craft over the side, it filled with water. One crewman, perhaps braver than the rest, jumped in anyway and bailed furiously. When the boat was sufficiently water free, three others joined their mate in bailing water.

Reciprocity had struck head on and the jib-boom and bowsprit were smashed. Once the crew thought of abandoning the wreck, it was too late for them to get below to save any clothes or personal belongings. All they could do was row off in the lifeboat and watch.

To their amazement another squall of wind buffeted the schooner and as the mainsail and foresail were still up, the schooner swung free of the ledge. *Reciprocity*, with no one aboard, went straight up Freshwater Bay as fine as if it had a full crew manning the wheel and sails. The crew quickly unshipped all oars and rowed after their vessel, but soon realized it was useless to try and overtake it.

By this time the harbour tug *D.P. Ingraham* appeared on the scene and in the nick of time. Another shift in wind was driving the lifeboat out to sea and the men could not row against the wind and tide. Clearly though they saw *Reciprocity* drive up Freshwater Bay, run ashore and fall over on its side. Almost immediately the spars fell and the schooner broke up.

Captain Blackmore and his six men had only the clothes they stood in; others lost their cash. The captain lost twenty-five dollars stored in his trunk, plus the five dollars in his pants pocket along with his watch. The other crew lost their money which totalled 200 dollars between them.

In the cloud of calamity there was a silver lining: the crew considered themselves lucky to be alive for had the wreck occurred at night, they felt they would have all drowned. As well the schooner was insured in the Wesleyville insurance scheme and could be replaced.

Tug *D.P. Ingraham* brought the men into St. John's where they made arrangements for transportation back home.

A ROUND-ABOUT TRIP FROM ST. PIERRE

Captain Edward Hounsell and mate Edward Davis belonged to Newtown, Bonavista Bay, and were once employed on the tern schooner *Pelleen*. In early December 1924 Hounsell hoisted *Pelleen*'s sails to head for Port au Port, intending to load lumber for Corner Brook. However, he and his crew ended up on the French Islands on Newfoundland's south coast.

Captain Job Kean's schooner *Daisy Kean* moored at Brookfield, Bonavista Bay, with Kean's store right. Virtue Kean ran this store for years.

Pelleen, a 431-ton ship with an overall length of 145 feet and owned by Arthur House of Port au Port, was only five years old. It had been built in Port Blandford. Indeed the name *Pelleen* is derived from the name of the main shipwright, D. Pelley.

With the exception of the captain and mate, most of the crew belonged to Port au Port. All that year the schooner worked in the lumber and coastal trade mainly from Port au Port, North Sydney, and Bell Island.

On December 9, while in the Gulf of St. Lawrence, a typical December storm with a strong north west gale lashed *Pelleen*, driving it back into Cabot Strait and toward St. Pierre. Davis decided to harbour on the French islands, but in the high winds, the schooner stranded on Miquelon and went to pieces. The crew made land with incident and went to the island's largest town, St. Pierre, where transportation was more readily available.

All crew went by steamer to Sydney, Nova Scotia. The men who belonged to Port au Port took a passage to Port aux Basques, while the captain and mate waited to join the steamer *Sable I*. On Christmas Eve, both men reached St. John's and arranged for transportation to Bonavista Bay and home.

Chapter 18

Action at Cabot Islands

A long Newfoundland's south coast, the bankers fished the offshore banks in spring, summer, and fall and, during the winter months, carried island goods to the markets of the Caribbean, United States, and Europe. The Northeast coast had its schooners too, but most of them were heavily involved in a somewhat different, but equally valuable sort of trade. Each spring, many went to the ice to hunt seals, and later headed north to the Labrador fishery. Each fall, the schooners went to St. John's to unload the summer's catch and to carry home the supplies needed to survive winter in the isolated communities along the coast.

These voyages, usually made in November or early December, were the most dangerous. Gales swept the North Atlantic and skippers had to be more vigilant to avoid the navigational hazards, mostly small islands and reefs, strewn along the Northeast coast.

Cabot Islands, two islets, are situated five and a half miles southeast by south off Cape Freels and about eight miles east by north of Swains Tickle, Bonavista Bay. Cabot Islands are listed in the 1901 census with eleven people, but these were probably the lighthouse keepers and their families for there was never a permanent town on the islands. In the era of the extensive inshore cod fishery, the waters adjacent these islands were good fishing locales.

Schooners plied the coastlines adjacent to the islands going to and from Conception Bay, Trinity Bay, Bonavista Bay, Greenspond or Catalina to the lucrative Labrador fishing grounds or on trading missions to and from St. John's. Since the islands are near oft-travelled routes, shipwrecks and human disasters were frequent. For example, the schooner *Puritan* was wrecked on Cabot Islands in December 1899 and the *Majestic*, under skipper Arch Roberts, was abandoned off Cabot Islands on December 10, 1906.

One of the more recent wrecks was the auxiliary vessel *James Jones*, a coaster built in 1936 and re-built in 1945 at Pool's Island by Jessie Hunt. In 1951 it was owned by Captain Chesley Dyke of Pool's Island who sold the schooner the next year to the Atlantic Shipping Company of St. John's. The following story demonstrates again the assistance and generosity of the people of the area — Cabot Islands, Pinchard's Island, Wesleyville — who came to the rescue.

On Sunday, August 31, 1952, while eight miles off Cape Bonavista, Captain Collins discovered a fire in the engine room of 104-ton *James Jones*. He soon found there was no time to retrieve any personal belongings as fire gained momentum in the oil-soaked compartment. Flames enveloped the schooner, and by the time the dory was hastily launched off deck, they were leaping mast high.

As the crew struggled with the dory, an explosion ripped out the inside of *James Jones*, now drifting out of control. The dory had to be put out on the windward side.

Collins and his four crew attempted to row to Bonavista, but were forced to run before a strengthening southwest gale. Eighteen hours later, tired and exhausted, they reached Cabot Islands and beached on the sea-girt island. Alex Gill, the island light keeper, gave them every care and consideration. To let the towns on the mainland know there had been a shipwreck, he hoisted a distress flag.

On Tuesday, September 2, in response to the signal, Captain Lloyd Hann left Wesleyville in the M.V. *Redwing Chief* to determine why the distress flag was up on the island. The shipwrecked men, exhausted after battling the elements, decided not to board the *Redwing Chief*, but to stay another day to recuperate.

They were eventually brought to Newtown by Bert Gill, Alex Gill's brother, of Pinchard's Island. The stranded crew was taken to Gambo on *Redwing Chief* to catch the train to their homes.

Fifteen months later on December 2, 1953, the *Redwing Chief* was destroyed by fire at Hermit Cove, Bonavista Bay.

Wreck of *Adhern Trader* (above). On January 5, 1960, the 774-ton steamer *Ahern Trader* grounded at Frederickton, Notre Dame Bay. It was built in 1922 and had operated around Newfoundland waters for many years. Its hulk remains there today. Photo courtesy of Garry Cranford.

Chapter 19

The Memory of Little Jap

Deer Island/Fair Island/Gooseberry Islands/Glovertown

In the early days of sail when there was no ship-to-shore or wireless communications, once a vessel went out of sight of land, nothing more was known of its whereabouts or condition until it returned, or had been "spoken to" by another vessel. Then, perhaps, another ship brought some news to home port. Shipowners, families, and loved ones could only wait hoping that, after a schooner left, the men would return days, weeks, or even months later.

Towns that sent their ships down to reap the sea's bountiful goods often paid the ultimate price for the ocean's riches and all too often the words "Lost with Crew" are noted beside a roster of ships. Usually in the lists of lost ships in Newfoundland and Labrador, the victims are not, as one would expect, the fishing vessels. Rather most ships and lives were taken in the coasting trade; that is those vessels that brought cured fish and supplies to and from larger centres. Along Newfoundland's south coast the large centre was often Sydney, Halifax or Prince Edward Island. In Conception Bay, Trinity Bay, Notre Dame Bay, and Bonavista Bay the larger centre was St. John's.

One of the ships that sailed away to St. John's never to return was the schooner *Little Jap* of Deer Island, Bonavista Bay, skippered by John Feltham. It was a vessel of about sixty tons used in the Labrador fishery. In the spring, summer, and early fall, the Felthams of Deer Island went to Labrador, fished, and returned home just before winter.[1] In late October or early November, vessels like *Little Jap* carried their salt dried fish to St. John's and returned with basic food supplies for the long winter. In this case, men from other Bonavista Bay islands made the trip to purchase food, clothing, and supplies for their respective island homes.

Little Jap left Deer Island on November 9, 1909, with thirteen men aboard — most were from Deer Island.[1,2] With favourable winds, and if the ship did not harbour overnight along the way, the run could be made in twelve to fifteen hours. Wednesday morning, several hours after *Little Jap* left, a typical November storm came up, intensified, and waned by the next day. Other schooners out in the same storm experienced difficulties but weathered the storm. *Little Jap* had a seasoned crew and should not have been adversely affected. They knew how to handle a vessel in rough weather. They also knew the sunkers, reefs, and headlands and should have navigated them safely.[1]

At least one other schooner came near to being lost with crew: Captain Martin Bishop of Wesleyville in *Beacon Light* met the gale head on. Its main boom broke and part of it fell on Japhet Mullett breaking his leg. Realizing *Beacon Light* was out of control and in danger of drifting on the rocks, Bishop ordered up the distress flags. Fortunately the S.S. *Louise* saw the signals, got a cable aboard and towed the wallowing schooner into Catalina. Captain Bishop said after, "There is little doubt but for the steamer *Louise*, the *Beacon Light* would have gone to the bottom with fourteen men aboard."[3]

But what of *Little Jap*? Days passed and nothing was heard of its whereabouts. No other vessel had seen or "spoken to" the *Little Jap*. No message came from St. John's telling loved ones of a safe arrival and there was no word they had reached any port.

On November 23, 1909, brief articles in the *Evening Telegram* and *Daily News* raised the possibility *Little Jap* had been lost with crew. Reports said that if the vessel was gone, it would be an overwhelming tragedy for Deer Island. There was no cause or reason given for its loss although the prevalent theory among the Bonavista Bay island people at the time was that it had collided with another vessel of unknown identity. It is quite possible the storm on the night it left put the little ship to grief on Gooseberry Islands. Some debris had been found there after the storm abated.

Wreckage had also been found in King's Cove, Bonavista Bay. In an air of uncertainly and desperation, a telegram sent from Bonavista Bay to the Honorable Sydney Dara Blandford read:

> Vessel dismasted, full of water and floating off. Supposed to be *Little Jap* of Deer Island. Left that place Tuesday November 9 for St. John's and has not been since heard of. Supposed to been lost in storm on Wednesday November 10. Fourteen souls aboard. Wreck now in vicinity of Western Point, King's Cove.

The author of *Wind and Wave* at the plaque dedicated to the loss of the Deer Island schooner *Little Jap*. It is located opposite the United Church, Glovertown, and overlooks the sea.

This debris was thought to belong to Tiller's schooner *Valkyrie* which sailed out of Newtown and stranded in the storm without loss of life. The paper erred in number of men aboard *Little Jap*; there were actually thirteen.[4]

The Deer Island men lost on *Little Jap* were skipper John Feltham, age thirty, who left a wife and four children, the oldest at age seven. Benjamin Feltham, his brother, was thirty-one and not married. The Deer Island schoolteacher Arthur King, thirty, left a wife and two sons. Born in St. John's, he was married to the skipper's sister. Charles Feltham, fifty-one, left a wife and four children and Abraham Feltham forty-eight, left a wife and five children. He and Charles were cousins of the skipper.

Samuel and George Boland were from Fair Islands and Jacob Sturge, Bragg's Island. Four belonged to Gooseberry Island: Robert Payne, age twenty-two; Thomas Taylor, twenty; Cator James House, age twenty-six and Absalom J. House, twenty-three.[1,2,5]

The latter two were the youngest sons of Job and Harriett House. In 1906, Cator married Eliza Saunders in the Anglican Church of St. Albans, Gooseberry Island, and they had a son, Laurence Gladstone House born in June 1909. He was five months old when his father drowned on *Little Jap*. On the marriage certificate Cator's name is written very clearly "Cator Howse," although in most references and on a memorial plaque (see author's note below) it is spelled House.

Job and Harriett House had three sons. Their eldest, Walter Wesley House, had gone to Vancouver and worked in a herring factory. He drowned a couple of years prior to the loss of *Little Jap*. The triple drowning in two different incidents left Job and Harriett House with no immediate family. Job eventually left Gooseberry Islands and went to live in Hare Bay with his nephew James House.[5]

Author's note and sources: In the summer of 2002, I visited Glovertown, Bonavista Bay, a town which received many families from the islands of Bonavista Bay during the era of resettlement. On Glovertown's main street and near the town's war memorial, I inadvertently located the plaque dedicated to the lost ship "Little Jap" and the thirteen men who sailed on it. It was situated in a park/rest area overlooking the bay with a grove of young pine trees as a backdrop — a very peaceful and serene setting when one considers the violent end to the schooner and its thirteen occupants.

Surely, I thought, the people of the islands, although they had left their homes where generations had lived, worked and prospered, did not want to forget the crew of *Little Jap*. The memorial tablet and inscription helps keep the memory alive. It motivated me to find out more of the loss. To that end the following references are noted: 1. Feltham, Jack. *The Islands of Bonavista Bay*. Harry Cuff Publications, St. John's, 1986; 2. Inscription on Memorial Tablet, Glovertown; 3. Unidentified newspaper article November 20, 1909; 4. *Evening Telegram*, November 23, 24, 25 and *Daily News*, November 23, 1909; 5. House, Domino. Notes on Cator and Absalom House (Howse), 2002.

No Tidings of *Little Jap* Two weeks after the ship left port concern for its whereabouts appears in Newfoundland papers.

The anchor and name board for a schooner built in 1935 in Glovertown, a busy shipbuilding centre throughout its history. In 1935-36, during the Commission of Government's bounty incentive for shipbuilding, scores of schooners large and small were built in Newfoundland.

In mid-July 1946, *M.V. New Hope*, en route to St. John's with a cargo of barrels of herring and birch junks, capsized in Baccalieu Tickle. It was towed into Harbour Grace by the dredge *Priestman*, working at Port-de-Grave.

Fortunately for owner/captain Nelson Burry of Glovertown and his three crew another schooner, *Beatrice and Vera May*, was following close behind *New Hope*. Captain Snow picked up the crew and carried them to St. John's.

Chapter 20

A Big Schooner: R.R. Govin

Glovertown/Grand Bank/St. John's/Labrador

The four-masted *R.R. Govin* was large compared to most Newfoundland schooners. Designed and built to carry lumber on the eastern seaboard of the United States, it netted 872 tons and had an overall length of 186 feet. The average tonnage of most island schooners was between fifty to 100 tons.

R. R. Govin (above) at San Juan, Puerto Rico in 1937. Shortly after *Govin* arrived in Newfoundland, the forepole and fore topsail were removed. The vessel, fastened with iron bolts, had an unusual feature for a Newfoundland schooner. It had two decks: a main top deck, a middle deck and below that the fish hold. Photo courtesy of Herb Thomasen.

In 1935, W. (Wilfred) Wareham's fish exporting business, based in Harbour Buffett, Placentia Bay, purchased *R.R. Govin*, and put it under the command of Captain Alex Rodway of Kingwell, Placentia Bay. After a few short voyages, Wareham decided the vessel was too large to operate economically and its registry passed to Monroe's business of St. John's.

Two men who fondly recall the *Govin*, as the schooner came to be known, are Nelson Oram of Glovertown and Norman Chaytor of St. John's. He served as cook on the *Govin* in the spring of 1938.

Oram, who fished on the Labrador coast from 1929 to 1949, remembers seeing *R.R. Govin* for the first time at Long Tickle, Labrador. "That summer, I think it was 1935, I was part of a group of thirty-two men who lived on board the schooner *Lucy Kemp*, a floating bunk-cook house."

The next summer Nelson Oram joined the fishing crew of the *Govin* and boarded his ship about four miles off Greenspond Island as it was on its way to the Labrador fishery from St. John's. "I was sixteen years old," he recalls, "and it was Sunday morning, June 21, 1936, when I went aboard the *Govin*." Others with him were his father Edward Oram, Charles Oram, Henry Oram (often called Little Henry), and Robert Lane, all of Bragg's Island. He went on to say:

> We went to meet the *R.R. Govin* in a little two mast-ed schooner *Bridget Kennedy* run by sail and a six-teen horsepower Acadia gas engine. My half brother John looked after this vessel for Monroe Export Company. We picked up Samuel Cooze and another man at Greenspond to bring *Bridget Kennedy* back to Bragg's Island after we boarded the *Govin*.
>
> We knew the *Govin* had left St. John's because a telegram arrived at Bragg's Island saying:
>
> *Govin leaving St. John's. Be ready to meet at Greenspond, Puffin Island, in two-three days.*

Photo of crew in January 1938 as *R.R. Govin* prepares to leave Halifax for England with a cargo of lumber. Crew (l-r): Philip Stone, age twenty-seven, Fortune Bay; Frank Witherall, twenty-nine, Fortune; Tom Coffin, twenty, St. John's; Captain Harry Thomasen, forty, Grand Bank; Rae Hadley, twenty, Cole Harbour, Guysboro, Nova Scotia; bosun Harold Samson, thirty-one, Grand Bank; cook Norman Chaytor, nineteen, St. John's; and mate John Ralph, thirty-nine, Grand Bank. Navigator Henry Burke, age sixty-nine, a native of Lunenburg, Nova Scotia, joined the crew just before the ship sailed and is missing from photo.

Others already aboard who had worked on the great ship in St. John's were Nelson's half brothers, John and Henry Oram, Nathan Rogers of Bragg's Island, Jim and John Paul, Green's Island, and Eli Feltham of Deer Island. For the summer's fishing expedition, Captain John Dominey had on board, including the crew, sixty-three men. "We received," Oram says, "thirty-five dollars a month. There was no charge for food and lodging."

Oram remembered other crew: Don and Leo McCarthy, Placentia Bay; Eddie and Don Snow, Carbonear; Arthur and Baxter Ford, two brothers from Wesleyville; Baxter's son; and a man named Halfyard.

The sixty-three crew lived aboard the great schooner. Oram recalls the middle deck with its eating space and the rooms for sleeping quarters. Six men were assigned to a room each with a bunk and a proper mattress — a far cry from the mattresses filled with feathers, goose grass or shavings used on small local schooners. Food — fresh meat, birds, vegetables and on Sundays oranges, apples and prunes — was brought from the galley to the forecastle. The crew could eat and work under electric lights supplied by a small steam generator. Oram recalled:

> The *Govin* anchored at Long Tickle and we fished with cod traps. We landed our catch aboard the schooner right from the trap. Fish was put in rope bags, tied to the side of the ship in the water to keep it cold and fresh, and hoisted aboard as needed. It was then cut, split, cleaned and salted in the holds. Only dip nets were used as fish forks would damage the fish.

> *R.R. Govin* was actually a "floating fish plant" as Oram remembers. In the hold were two tracks for the hand-pushed trolley to carry salt or fish. In the holds fish was salted and stored in pounds; large fish on one side, small ones on the other.

> Other fishing crews under charter to Monroe Export Company brought their catch to the side of *R.R. Govin* for processing: from Iron Bound Island, Manrock Tickle, Strawberry Harbour and Dunns Island. Altogether the *Govin* was supplied with round codfish from thirty-six traps which caught about 500 quintals a day. On board the ship there were ten splitting tables, three men each and five or six salters. After three weeks at Long Tickle, it moved to Makkovik where the schooner *C & A Brown* offloaded 1,500 quintals. This was taken to Badger's Quay to be dried in the open air.

> Later in the summer when fish became scarce, the *Govin* moved to Little St. Juliens near St. Anthony where the crew fished from baited trawls. Later at St. Juliens a small steamer, commanded by Captain Bragg, carried more fish to Badger's Quay.

Rita Blanche House (above) had a Glovertown connection: it was built in the 1930s on the town's north shore and owned by Edgar House of Glovertown. In 1939, the schooner was used in the Labrador fishery, but was later sold to Charles Dowden, Wesleyville/Pound Cove. In turn he sold it to Captain Fred Pickett, Fair Island, Bonavista Bay. *Rita Blanche House* was lost near Musgrave Harbour with a load of salt. Photo Courtesy of Nelson Oram.

In the last week of October, *R.R. Govin* sailed for Carbonear. Nelson Oram and his father found a ride to St.

John's on a truck and stayed aboard one of Monroe's tern schooners for three nights. Skipper Patrick Furlong (Sr.) was headed to St. Brendan's, Bonavista Bay, so "we went with him and from there to Bragg's Island in a motor boat. We made 320 dollars for both of us from late June to October."

In 1938, while the *Govin* was on a foreign-going voyage, its crew had a memorable battle with the sea. On January 27, it left Halifax for Liverpool with a cargo of lumber. Sailing went well until it ran into an Atlantic storm off England. For twenty days, until March 1, *R.R. Govin* was battered and beaten, but stayed afloat because it was filled with lumber. The weary crew (as shown on page 96) pumped continuously and finally made Loch-in-Dale, Scotland. The pump mates were: mate Ralph and cook Chaytor, Captain Thomasen and Hadley, Samson and Coffin, Witherall and Stone. After *Govin* was repaired, it sailed for home and arrived in Newfoundland on June 27, 1938.

R.R. Govin ended its days on the coast of the Labrador. In the fall of 1939, it went to Snug Harbour, buying salt fish and supplying fishermen. On October 26, it struck a reef off Snug Harbour while leaving port and sank with 1,200 quintals aboard. The pumps couldn't keep it free; the *Govin* was set afire. The spars and top decks burned out in two days. The wreckage, mainly the bottom of the hull, drifted ashore.

On the same day the *Govin* was lost, another schooner, *W. G. Robertson* owned by Robert Guy of Catalina, burned off Elliston. Guy and his crew rowed into Catalina.

Chapter 21

Friendly Fire: H.M.S. Patricia Rammed

Charleston/Charlottetown, Bonavista Bay

By 1915, England and its allies were embroiled in a global war on land and at sea against Germany. Many young seamen, from nearly every town and bay in Newfoundland, came forward to serve. One thousand five hundred enlisted in the Royal Navy and of these 180 were killed or drowned.

In its reference to Newfoundlander sailors in the Naval Service, the *Cambridge History of the British Empire* says, "The seamen of Newfoundland had long been known in the Navy as efficient and resourceful, but the end of the War left them with a greatly enhanced reputation. They readily undertook almost impossible boarding operations in wild seas which others would not face. Nothing but praise was accorded by the Fleet."

These were the young and married men who normally would have been fishing, farming or providing income for family at home, but chose to join the Royal Navy and to serve on British ships in the war at sea. Many historians claim that part of the cause of Newfoundland's economic woes in the 1930s was because its youth and leadership had been decimated on the killing fields of Europe.

Edgar Quinton of Charleston, Bonavista, signed up and in time was assigned to the H.M.S. *Patricia*, a British navy ship patrolling the North Sea. Located at the head of Southern Bay in Bonavista Bay, Charleston gets its name from an early settler, Charles Quinton, who moved to Southern Bay from Pinchard's Point, about ten miles up the shore. Lovell's *Newfoundland Directory* of 1871 lists Charles Quinton and James Quinton as planters of Southern Bay, and Breen, Gould, McCormack, Moss, Prince, White and Yetman as fishermen.

OTHER TOWNS SENT THEIR YOUTH TO WAR AS WELL, AS EVIDENCED BY THIS SONG:

HERRING NECK'S PATRIOTISM

Come all young men of Newfoundland
And listen unto me,
Of eight young men of Herring Neck,
Who are fighting on the sea.

The first young man to answer
The Motherland's great call,
His name is Chesley Kearley,
And he is fighting for us all.

The next young man to volunteer,
From Too-Good-Arm he came,
A little place in Herring Neck,
Darius Hurley is his name.

He is his parents only son,
And they thought it hard to part
From him who was the dearest,
Of a fond mother's heart.

Then Patrick Woodford said,
"I'll be a soldier from the Bight
And go over to fair Flanders,
And fight for what is right."

"And now," said Moses Burton
To Philip Blandford, brave,
"Let's show that we're not slow
For our King and Country save."

So three more men in Herring Neck
said, "We will not be slow,
Through fire, smoke, shot and shell,
Unto the war we'll go."

Their names are Eric Woodford,
And Chesley Miles, likewise,
And then Oliver H. Batt.
They're all plucky boys.

So come young men, be British.
Don't fill a coward's grave;
But be one of those sailor boys
Who are both bold and brave.

"A Lover of Patriotism"
Herring Neck, May 24, 1916

The early economy of Charleston was based on fishing, farming, and boat building. Its location made the community an excellent farming centre, and agriculture was a full-time occupation for many inhabitants from the 1890s to the 1920s. By 1911, Charleston had the largest area of cultivated land from Open Hall to Bloomfield. The main crops were turnip and cabbage, and sheep, pigs, goats, horses, and cows were raised. Lumbering and family-owned sawmills contributed to the town's economy. With a small population base, Charleston, like most Newfoundland towns, could ill afford to lose able-bodied men from its work force during the Great War.

A Bonavista Bay schooner *Doris G. Samson* (above). Built in Lunenburg in 1916, *Ella Mason* was purchased in Newfoundland. After it was rebuilt by Art Samson of Flat Islands, Bonavista Bay, the schooner was renamed *Doris G. Samson*. In the photo, the seventy-four-ton *Doris G. Samson* crosses Barnes Bay, Labrador, in 1942 with Skipper Harold Ralph, Glovertown, in command. Photo courtesy of Nelson Oram, Glovertown.

Edgar Quinton of Charleston recalled his action during the Great War and, in one skirmish, Quinton remembered that his vessel was nearly sunk by "friendly fire."

On Monday, July 12, 1915, *Patricia* left a port in England to report for duty in the North Sea. On Wednesday about midnight, crewmen on *Patricia* sighted another ship bearing down toward them. According to Quinton:

> We signaled for it to stop, but instead of stopping, the vessel came straight toward us, striking us a very heavy blow in the starboard bow, smashing up one of our guns.
>
> We got out the collision mat over the hole and prevented a greater inrush of water, but we were in a sinking condition for a long while. But in less than three hours we had four or five of our own ships standing by and they managed to get us fitted up enough to reach port. We had to have thirty-six plates of steel put in our bow. You can easily imagine what kind of a blow it was.
>
> However we put the other ship that rammed us snug in its grave. We rescued the crew all right and we saw them safe enough in another British ship, the *Digby*.

Edgar Quinton finished his story, saying he and shipmates had been in several scraps, but came out of all of them without mishap. Eventually the damaged *Patricia* was ready for sea again. Unfortunately one of his friends — Heber Chaulk of Charlottetown, Bonavista Bay — ended up in hospital in Chatham, England, but Quinton reported that his condition was improving.

Other Newfoundlanders on H.M.S. *Patricia* were George Snow of Bay Roberts; Fred Stead, Catalina; John Soper, Lady Cove, Trinity Bay; A. Power, Placentia; G. Janes and Vincent Dobbin, Upper Island Cove; Isaac Keefe, Twillingate; Roland Heath and Joseph Anstey, Pilley's Island; J.P. Taylor, Alexander Bay; James Hayes, Brigus; and three whose residence was given only as Trinity Bay, Eloil Baker, W. Smith, and George Matthews.

On October 3, 1910, during a northeast storm, the 100-ton Danish schooner *Kronen* parted its moorings off Bonavista and, in the night, drifted onto the Canaille shore. At 8 a.m. the men of Bonavista saw the plight of the crew and in the height of the gale, James Ford, William Ford, Eli Paul, William Reader, Copald Way, and William Russell rescued *Kronen*'s crew. Bonavista's Magistrate John Roper reported the wreck to the Deputy Minister of Customs in St. John's, H.W. LeMessurier.

In December 2002, Steen Jorgensen, the grandson of *Kronen*'s Captain Hans Frederik Carl Hermansen (inset), called me to learn more of the wreck. In the exchange of information, Steen sent me the photo of *Kronen* (above).

Chapter 22

The Price of Coal

The coal trade between Newfoundland and Nova Scotia lasted approximately 100 years. Beginning around the 1850s, vessels from Newfoundland regularly visited North Sydney for coal. Extensive coal mining and exportation began in Nova Scotia about 1850 when vast amounts of coal were needed to fuel Canadian locomotives and steamships. By this time in the development of Newfoundland towns, many stands of trees and firewood close to communities had been depleted. North Sydney coal had replaced wood as fuel, especially in the larger centres like St. John's. A hundred years later, 1940-50s, small coasting schooners of Newfoundland were still loading coal at North Sydney.

But the price of coal paid for in sunken ships and lost lives was great. It is not the intention here to recount the losses of many colliers, or coal carriers. Wooden ships were often overloaded and carried coal on deck, seams opened and pumps failed or clogged with coal dust. The treacherous Gulf of St. Lawrence was at its worst in the fall of the year when many Newfoundland vessels voyaged to Nova Scotia. In storms there was always a danger of the coal shifting and causing a list; thus it had to be loaded, or trimmed, with great care.

Explosions caused by coal were not uncommon aboard Newfoundland schooners. Apparently when "slack" or dusty coal was loaded, the fine dust could ignite from spontaneous combustion or from friction. To reduce the likelihood of explosions captains gave dusty coal lots of ventilation. Some skippers kept a hatch cover loose. Other types of coal — harder or in large pieces — were not as prone to explode. The story is told of the vessel *Nellie Cluett*, a Newfoundland schooner moored in Sydney harbour, which exploded as a result of coal dust in the holds. A nurse aboard was slightly injured.

George B. Cluett (above), one of the largest fishing schooners built in Lunenburg, Nova Scotia. *George B. Cluett* struck St. Paul's Island which lies about nine miles off Cape Breton's northernmost tip.

Beginning about 1930, *George B. Cluett* had a long and distinguished career serving the Labrador coast under the registry of the Grenfell Mission. In 1940, it was sold to a business in Newfoundland. Ken Iverson skippered the vessel in the ten years with the Grenfell Mission while it was based out of St. Anthony. Photo courtesy of Hubert Hall, SHIPSEARCH Marine.

While on the way to Quebec with coal on October 7, 1941, the 198-ton *George B. Cluett* struck a reef off St. Paul's Island while proceeding slowly in dense fog. Captain Robert Guy of Catalina and his crew stayed on the craft until the hatches were under water and then scrambled aboard the lifeboat. As Guy recalled:

We waited until daybreak to find out where we were. When we saw land we rowed ashore and landed near St. Paul's Island wireless station. Later we were taken off the island and brought to Dingwall, from where we were carried to North Sydney by the fishing schooner *Marion and Rita* of North Sydney.

In addition to Captain Guy, *George B. Cluett*'s other crew were mate John T. Hiscock, engineer Henry Norman, Edward Mullins, Herbert Jerrett, Joseph McKay and Tobias Ivany. It is believed that the schooner was later salvaged, repaired, and lived to sail again. Ironically it sank again off St. Paul's Island in 1942. Today it is a favourite locale for divers searching for wrecks off St. Paul's.

Built in 1920 at Conquerall Bank, Nova Scotia, the 148-ton *Retraction* (above) was owned by Philip Templeman of Bonavista. In February 1926, it was abandoned at sea while returning from Spain. The crew, Captain John Sinclair and his brother mate Max Sinclair hailed from St. John's while the rest of its crew were from Bonavista Bay and area: bosun Maxwell House and cook Simon Stead of Catalina, Abner Brenson, Bonavista and Harry White of Harcourt, Trinity Bay.

    Retraction sailed from Cadiz, Spain, on New Year's Eve of 1925, but as January of the new year progressed, the tern encountered a tremendous southwesterly gale. In the wild seas, the deck heaved, opened the seams, and *Retraction* filled with water that no amount of pumping could keep out.

    On February 5, a tanker, *El Oso* bound for Curacao in the Dutch West Indies, rescued the crew. Photo courtesy of Lance Blackmore, Port Union/Grand Bank.

Of course, there is always the prospect of salvage when the coal carriers are stranded and abandoned near the shore. Take the case of the *Ruth Adams* and Captain Alex Elms when his schooner ran aground on Point aux Gaul Point on September 29, 1944. The residents of Point aux Gaul, located a few miles northeast of Lamaline on the Burin Peninsula, cheerfully brought home handtubs of coal to be stored for winter's burning. One old lady reportedly spoke to the captain saying, "Thank God for this. 'Tis an ill wind that doesn't blow somebody good and we got our coal for the winter." The vessel was a total wreck.

Chapter 23

A Wreck on Elliston's Shores

Captain Thomas Kean of St. Brendan's, Bonavista Bay, owned and skippered the fifty-seven-ton schooner *George A. Butler*. Kean, intending to get to home port before Christmas with his cargo of food and general supplies, left St. John's and harboured in Catalina the first night. This was the normal procedure for the coasting vessels of northern Newfoundland. Catalina was a day's run from St. John's even for the slowest schooner.

Kean left Catalina on December 22, 1937, for the final leg to St. Brendan's; however a storm forced him back to port. Captain Kean tried to get into Catalina, but that was impossible and he had to sail to Elliston. As the night came on, conditions deteriorated, forcing the crew to leave the schooner. It was under difficult circumstances they reached shore at Elliston.

Their home on the water was in danger and they had nowhere to stay, but Mr. E. Baker of Elliston took them in. The next day the crew went back to the schooner, made two attempts to get under way, but again the weather was too stormy.

By this time high seas — the highest Elliston people had seen in years — pounded the shoreline. The winds had increased to hurricane force. Any schooner not in safe anchorage would be in trouble. Kean anchored his vessel as best he could and again he and his crew left for safety of the shore.

At 3:30 p.m. Sunday, December 26, *George A. Butler* broke its chains, ran ashore, and such were the force of seas that within a few minutes the schooner had its back broken on the rocky shoreline. Nothing was saved and another fine schooner was reduced to debris near Elliston.

That unfortunate ending to a fine schooner was not as traumatic as the reports coming out of Greenspond of another wreck, this one more tragic. A mast, picked up near Roger's Point in Greenspond Tickle by William Jerrett, was brought to authorities by Captain Percy Knee of coastal steamer *Sagona*. The mast was thirty-one feet long, almost all of it scorched by fire.

According to a veteran seamen, this mute evidence had tell-tale signs of a shipwreck or sea disaster for it was broken off flush with the deck, had a two-band goose neck, and a piece of canvas was attached. Captain W. Pelley of Trinity Bay examined the material and believed it belonged the missing schooner *A. Hubley*. The debris had been found December 8, 1937.

The last time *A. Hubley* had been seen was on November 18, off Cape Bonavista by the Port Union motor vessel *Marie Yvonne*, Captain Walter Bragg. The *Hubley*, as it was commonly called in its home port of New Perlican, left Catalina on November 18, bound for the Grois Islands, near the tip of the Great Northern Peninsula. *Hubley* carried four crew: Captain "Neddie" Seward, his son Walter, his brother Mark and seaman Pierre Ross of St. John's.

By November 29, thoughts and fears for the safety of the men surfaced publically. As requested by the Newfoundland Railway, the steamer *Sagona* searched north of the Funk Islands in the belief that the missing ship may have drifted there. The revenue cutter *Marvita* searched off Fogo in good visibility, but there was no sign of *A. Hubley*. When Mr. Joshua Pitts, a relative of Captain

Seward, viewed the piece of damaged spar, he confirmed what many people thought.

By November 29, Newfoundland papers said "FEARS FOR SAFETY SCHR. A. HUBLEY: MISSING TEN DAYS"; eventually it was pronounced lost with crew.

GREEN ISLAND WRECK

One hundred and fifty tons of general freight went to the bottom near Green Island at the entrance to Catalina, a much-frequented harbour for vessels plying the coasting routes along Newfoundland's northeast coast.

In December 1894 the 1,934-ton steamer *Benisafe* was wrecked on a headland between Elliston and Bonavista. Captained by George Gundy and owned by C.T. Bowring of London, it left Pilley's Island for New York with a cargo of copper ore. The crew rowed into Spillard's Cove in two boats from *Benisafe*. Officers and crew lost everything in the wreck, but spoke in highest terms of the kindness and help they received at Bonavista and Elliston.

A port hole from *Benisafe* graced the "outhouse" door of Richard Baker (1881-1965) in Elliston for many years. When the need for exterior toilet facilities became outmoded, the porthole went into possession of his grandson Gary Crewe. Photo courtesy of Gary Crewe.

Early Wednesday morning on May 23, 1945, the sixty-seven-ton auxiliary vessel *Mazeltov* left St. John's.

Mazeltov, purchased by Horwood Lumber Company six years previously, carried supplies destined for Horwood and Fogo, as well as goods which would be taken overland to Gander. The coaster had been used during the summer months for towing logs to the Horwood Company mill at Horwood.

Due to heavy fog, Captain Stephen Goodyear of Carmanville misjudged his course while approaching Green Island. About 2:30 p.m. *Mazeltov* ran upon South East Shoal, a reef a short distance from the entrance to Catalina. The five-man crew and two passengers, Mr. and Mrs. Patrick Miller of Fogo, were landed safely in Catalina.

The pounding seas on Green Island soon made short work of the old workhorse; it quickly filled with water and became a total loss. Fortunately *Mazeltov* was covered by insurance.

Chapter 24

Loss of C. Bryant

Port Union/Burin

The Swedish steamer *Nuolja* sailed from Norvik, Norway, in late March 1927 with a cargo of iron ore for Port Richmond, New York. In the mid-Atlantic, the helmsman saw an unusual sight.

In the dark and gloom of 5:30 a.m. March 28, *Nuolja*'s Chief Officer Ohman saw a feeble flare, a light, bobbing on the horizon. It seemed to appear and disappear and looked like it was on the surface rather than from a mast or bridge of a ship. Hence, Ohman figured it couldn't be the light of a schooner or steamer. Finally he called Captain John Degerhalm.

Degerhalm later said,

> I thought at first it might be a gas buoy that had drifted from its mooring. I knew it could not be the light of a steamer because that is constantly in the line of visibility and would remain steady. We decided it must be an open boat and kept on our course towards it.

It was an open boat manned by Newfoundland sailors. The boat belonged to *C. Bryant*, a schooner out of Port Union, built by shipwright James "Jimmy" Jones and owned by the Fisherman's Trading Company. The castaways were Captain Frank Hollett, mate James Kirby, cook Levi Collins, all of Burin; Gerald Dillon, St. John's; Leo Walsh, Port Union; and Harry Russell, Catalina.

The museum at Port Union is filled with ship artifacts, photos and models of the Port Union Shipping Company. Two ship models, *C. Bryant* (top) and *Gull Pond* (bottom), on which Port Union shipwrights built the schooners.

Their little cockleshell of a craft, pitted against the mighty Atlantic, had been thirty hours adrift in the tail end of a gale. The gale still had enough fury that all six men believed the next descent into a trough of water might be their last. But they lived to tell about it, and Captain Hollett remembered it this way:

> We left Newfoundland in December 1926, with a cargo of fish for Pernambuco (now Recife), Brazil. On the way back we shipped a cargo of molasses at Barbados and set sail on March 22, 1927.
>
> We made good time with favourable wind until we were out five nights; then 350 miles northeast of Bermuda, the glass suddenly fell and we prepared for bad weather. It was one of the worst storms I ever experienced. For twenty-four hours high winds and choppy seas raged without abatement. Our schooner

C. Bryant was strained from stem to stern. After a day of pounding, seams opened and water poured into the hold.

Every man worked the pumps, trying to keep down the water that slowly gained on us. We could only hope for a fall of wind and seas so we could make some repairs. Twenty-four hours of steady pumping and no letup in the gale convinced us it was impossible to keep going. We would be lucky to get a lifeboat over the side.

At last we abandoned ship. We took water and food for a few days for we hoped we'd see a steamer and with that thought we kept up our spirits.

What Captain Hollett didn't know was that *C. Bryant* had been blown out of shipping lanes. *Nuolja*'s officers said they had not sighted a ship for three days before they saw the open boat and did not see another craft for three days after that.

It was a turn of the wheel a quarter point to starboard to put *Nuolja* back on course, but that slight turn of direction threw the steamer in the path of *C. Bryant*'s lifeboat.

At 1 a.m. on March 28, when cook Levi Collins saw the light of a steamer in the distance, Captain Hollett said, "We rowed as hard as we could towards it and we soon saw the ship was moving in a direction where it would pass near enough to see our signals." He continued:

We had some oil with us and we took off our shirts, soaked them in the oil, put them on oars and lighted them. We waved the oars in the air and the fire lit up the sky. After we signalled for what seemed like a long time, we saw the ship changed direction and was coming toward us.

The trials of six shipwrecked men were not over: the sea was still so high that the lifeboat could not make fast to the steamer. Instead *Nuolja*'s crew threw looped ropes to the small boat, standing off about forty feet away. One by one the six Newfoundland sailors fastened the ropes around their waist and were pulled aboard.

Certainly Captain Hollett had no illusions as to what his and his crew's fate would have been had the steamer not sighted them. They had three days worth of drinking water left and little food. If hunger or thirst had not claimed them, an angry sea certainly would have.

When they reached the United States, *C. Bryant*'s crew went to the office of the British consul, obtained a change of clothes and arranged for transportation back to Newfoundland.

As a footnote of marine stories, Frank Hollett of Great Burin, son of Captain Fred Hollett, was lost at sea less than a year later when the steamer *Sagua La Grande* disappeared in January 1928.

Two schooners sailing outside Port Union harbour: *G.& F. Blackmore* (left) and *A. & R. Martin* (right). *A. & R. Martin* was wrecked off Lamaline on December 12, 1951. *G.& F. Blackmore*, built about 1924 by Max Burry's shipyard in Glovertown, was named after Captain John H. Blackmore's sons, George and Fred Blackmore. Captain John of Port Union operated *G. & F. Blackmore* for sixteen years in the Labrador fishery before it was sold in Newfoundland. Its eventual fate is more obscure. Photo courtesy of Lance Blackmore.

Ryan Brothers' business, which originated in Bonavista in 1857, became one of the largest supply and fish exporting firms in Newfoundland. In 1906 the firm expanded to Trinity and soon grew to be that town's largest enterprise. The Trinity business closed on March 31, 1952.

Ryans' ships were engaged in the coastal and foreign trade and in the Labrador fishery. Their largest schooner, *Marguerite Ryan* (above locked in ice), a tern or three master used in the foreign-going trade to transport dry cod to the European market, was abandoned at sea in February 1923. Photo courtesy of Maritime History Archives.

Chapter 25

Twice Unlucky: M.V. Lutzen

Trinity/St. John's

When Job Brothers motor vessel *Lutzen* pulled into St. John's harbour on the night of Friday, January 9, 1937, it was under the command of mate Joseph Gullage. He had a tale of disaster to relate.

Laden with drums of oil and general cargo, the 339-ton *Lutzen* left Halifax for St. John's on Tuesday, January 5. Captain George Rideout steamed southeast to Egg Island, then changed course to east-southeast. At midnight, the wind veered to the west and the face of the sea changed — changed to heavy waves and this made for more dangerous sailing as seas broke across deck.

About 7 p.m. on Wednesday, the lifeboat broke from its lashings and banged around on deck. Three men ran out to secure the boat — Captain Rideout, Clifford Picco, and another sailor. The three tried to tie the lifeboat down again, but it gave a lurch and swung across the deck. The lifeboat went over the side taking the captain with it.

Immediately Picco grabbed a life buoy and threw it. Mate Gullage, who saw what had happened presumably from his position in the wheelhouse, ran out with a flashlight and aimed the beam near and around the lifeboat which was now dragging along *Lutzen*'s side attached by a rope.

Despite the attempts to find the captain he was not to be seen. *Lutzen* stayed in the area all night, searching the waters, but Captain Rideout was never found. Thursday morning at 8 a.m., the reluctant crew set *Lutzen's* course for St. John's and they arrived about 11 p.m. on Friday. Rideout was born in Port Union and was thirty-eight years old.

Two years later another tragedy touched *Lutzen*. In February 1939, it delivered frozen blueberries to New York. While approaching Cape Cod, Massachusetts, on February 3, it went aground and keeled over on the sands of Nauset Beach.

Two crew, Baxter Bailey and the mate, attempted to abandon the wreck by *Lutzen's* dory. In the surf the dory upset throwing both into the water. The mate survived but Bailey, aged twenty-eight and belonging to Trinity, Trinity Bay, drowned.

The men of the Old Harbor Lifeguard Station located near Cape Cod saw the *Lutzen's* difficulty and in time a surfboat was sent out to the wreck. The lifeguards rescued the remaining crew: Captain Robert J. Randell, C.R. Moore, James Gibbons, Arthur Amminson, Fred Candow, all of St. John's; Joseph Carey, Cape Broyle; and Clayton Pelley of Port Union.

Aground on the sand spit of Cape Cod in February 1939, the M.V. *Lutzen* lies a derelict. Although the ship was little damaged and the cargo was jettisoned in an attempt to refloat it, the motor vessel was declared a total wreck. In 1933 *Lutzen* was equipped with a 300 HP Fairbanks Morse Diesel engine and cold storage facilities. Photo courtesy of Hubert Hall, SHIPSEARCH Marine.

Crew of *Lutzen* landed by the Old Harbor Life Boat Crew. Captain Randell (man with hat on left) looks back at the stranded *Lutzen*. Photo courtesy of Hubert Hall, SHIPSEARCH Marine.

Chapter 26

Rescue at Point La Haye

Hickman's Harbour/Point La Haye

It has been estimated that thousands of vessels have been stranded and wrecked around the coasts of Newfoundland and Labrador. One area which has more claim to infamy when it comes to lost ships is the stretch of coast from Cape Race to St. Mary's Bay. In 1903, Mr. R. White, a St. John's resident, compiled a map of many Newfoundland wrecks. It shows the location of literally hundreds of the known wrecks at that time. In the region of the southern Avalon, there are so many ship names on it and all so close together there is scarcely room for any more. Yet there have been scores wrecked since the map was made.

The causes of these marine mishaps are many and varied — fog, unusual and powerful tides, hidden reefs, high volume of sea traffic, too few lighthouses and fog horns, and so on. Perhaps some of the causes can be combined and that seems to be the case for one small vessel wrecked in St. Mary's Bay in 1918, too late to be included on White's compilation. The schooner *Bessie R* battled winter winds and treacherous rocks, but in the end became a statistic for some future cartographer.

Bessie R left Bay Bulls with a cargo of salt for Port aux Basques and intended to load a cargo of fish at the latter port. It arrived in Fermeuse on the Southern Shore on Sunday, February 17, 1918, and its master, Sandy

Thistle, fully expected to harbour at Trepassey that night. However, once out and en route, the fickle forces of nature took command.

Thistle had an experienced crew; most like himself belonged to Hickman's Harbour on Random Island: mate Joseph T. Blundon (or Blundel), and Levi Benson. Cook John Anderson lived in British Harbour, but later moved to Britannia on Random Island. W. J. Peddle hailed from Little Heart's Ease and Lewis Rice from Bay Bulls. Joseph Peckford, a well-known citizen of St. John's, was super-cargo on the schooner. As supercargo he would have managed the business transactions of the *Bessie R*, whose main work seems to have been trading fish and supplies along the coast.

The skills of Thistle's crew were soon to be tried for the schooner ran headlong into a snow storm with south east winds. Within hours this swung round to a gale from the north west — the worst winds for sail driven vessels off southeastern Newfoundland. For twenty-four hours *Bessie R* was pushed to sea and during the gale the jumbo boom broke off. The log, towed on its line behind the ship which would give some indication of speed and distance, broke and Captain Thistle had no idea how far his schooner drifted off.

Slowly he and his crew worked the vessel back to within sight of land somewhere, as far as Thistle could determine, on the east side of St. Mary's Bay. By now, *Bessie R* was near a rock called by local folks, 'The Bull.' Thistle didn't recognize it at the time, but he did know that to save his vessel and possibly the lives of all aboard he needed to keep his schooner out to sea. Despite his best intentions, contrary winds pushed *Bessie R* near Holyrood Arm and there was no way to swing the schooner around to get out. The vessel made its last ditch stand off the town of Point LaHayse, or as it is known today, Gaskiers Point La Haye.

Although the roots of Point La Haye are with the early French fishery, the first English indication of the town appeared on Captain James Cook's 1762 map where it is noted as Point Le Hays. Point La Haye appears in the first official Newfoundland *Census* (1836) with a population of twenty-five, all Roman Catholic. In a later census the community shows as Gaskin Point, La Haye in reference to the well-populated town of Gaskiers nearby. In 1901, a lobster factory was established there and the fishery remained the mainstay of the town although many residents cultivated the land and kept livestock.

Residents of the town who bear namesakes of those who had settled there many years before include: Baldwin, Bishop, Cahill, Dobbin, Hayward, Meehan, Mooney, Francis, and Mandeville; later families of Rielly, Kielly, Tobin, and St. Croix arrived. No doubt it was people bearing these name sakes who saw the plight of the battered *Bessie R.*

As the schooner tacked about offshore, the people of Point La Haye gathered on a headland, watching the valiant efforts of six seamen. When *Bessie R* swung over with its bowsprit pointed directly at the land, they ran to the beach to help if they could. Feeling helpless and thinking that death could only result from such an undertaking, many knelt to ask the Good Lord to spare the lives of the struggling seamen.

At first, it seemed as if the schooner would ground and break up off shore. There seemed to be no recourse but disaster and death. One account of the wreck says: "The people on the shore never thought that any of the crew would reach land alive, and they gathered on the beach, praying for their safety."

But Captain Thistle drove *Bessie R* right up on the beach and the crew was able to jump off from the bowsprit to the shore much to the amazement of Point La Haye residents. Joseph Peckford sustained the only injury. During the two or three days of fighting the storm, Peckford had taken his turn at the wheel and bent over to examine the compass. The main boom swung, hit him in the middle of the back and his chest struck the wheel with considerable force. One of the wheel spokes injured his chest. The crew saved nothing but the clothes they stood in.

Despite their close call and two or three days of exciting and anxious hardships at sea, the crew, except businessman Peckford, went about their life work as mariners. They arrived in St. John's on February 28 on the coastal steamer *Glencoe*. Some of *Bessie R*'s seamen found work at Harbour Grace and went there to join *Henry L. Montague* for another stint on the ocean.

As for the wreck of *Bessie R*, there was not much left. It went to pieces and the debris was sold to James Bishop of Point La Haye for seven dollars.

This was not the last word on the wreck of *Bessie R*. Apparently one man was so impressed with the self-rescue of the hardy seamen, he wrote an unsigned letter to the *Evening Advocate*, dated March 11, 1918; the heading states: "NOTHING CAN DAUNT OUR BRAVE SEAMEN."

> Dear Sir: Please allow me space to say a few words about the loss of "Bessie R" at Point La Hayse, St. Mary's Bay, in one of the heaviest seas of thirty years and in the height of a winter storm. The ship ran ashore and everything was handled so well that every man was landed in twenty-five minutes in a way that no one but Newfoundland fishermen could do.
>
> My pen cannot tell you what a hero Mr. Joseph Peckford is. He nobly stayed to the wheel until the vessel grounded on the beach and the first place he was up to was the middle of the storm trysail which was set. If there are any medals to be given, those men deserve them. There are brave men in all ranks, but I think seamen beat them all.
>
> Another matter I would like to mention is that I think outport men might have a little more rum than men in the city. When you drag a man out of the surf the bottle seems mighty small

nowadays. I hope we will be able to get some more.

Yours very truly,
"A Good Hand to Throw a Line"
Point La Hayse, St. Mary's

Chapter 27

A Letter of Appeal

St. Jones Within, Trinity Bay

The Trinity Bay lumbering/fishing community, St. Jones Within, is located on the north side of Southwest Arm, approximately fifteen miles southeast of Clarenville. The town was an important woods operation site as early as the 1830s. It is not known why "saint" was added to the community name, but the "within" distinguishes the harbour from the other St. Jones, just outside Southwest Arm.

St. Jones Within was settled in the 1860s and 1870s, like other communities within Southwest Arm, largely by people from the Grates Cove area or from Bishop's Cove, Conception Bay. St. Jones Within first appears in the *Census* in 1869 with a population of fourteen people. There were sixty-five people by 1874.

Nearly all the early settlers were Methodists, including Simeon King, Hezekiah Benson, and Benjamin Squires, who were all residents by 1884. The well-protected harbour offered close access to inshore fishing grounds on the north side of the Arm and was used as a winter harbour for Labrador schooners. In addition, there have been several small sawmills at St. Jones Within.

Over the years, several families were resettled to St. Jones Within from nearby town of Loreburn. In 1994, common family names of the community includee Meadus and Price (from Loreburn), as well as Brown,

Holloway, King, Robbins, and Tucker. Not many sea stories are associated with St. Jones Within. Over the years
the town produced much lumber, but one marine misadventure describes the hazards of delivering the lumber to
St. John's and getting back home.

In the June 5, 1915, issue of *The Mail and Advocate*,
there appeared an appeal to the public to help Skipper
Matthais King. It begins with a general entreaty:

> Dear Sir: I regret to inform you that a friend met with
> a most serious loss last night in Conception Bay
> which again emphasizes the perils which our men
> have to face in the attempt to earn a living for them-
> selves and families. . .

The writer, the Chairman of the Carbonear Council,
went on to say,

> Skipper Matthais King in his schooner *Lily Beatrice*
> of St. Jones Within, Southwest Arm, Trinity Bay, left
> St. John's at 4 a.m. Tuesday morning, May 25, and
> made good progress to Cape St. Francis. There he
> hauled up Conception Bay to get around a string of
> ice and, while reaching to the eastward of Low Point
> north shore of Conception Bay, during thick fog,
> struck a large pan of ice.
>
> It staved in the port bow. *Lily Beatrice* filled with
> water and sank in less than ten minutes. The crew of
> four jumped upon a pan of ice just as they stood. They
> were fortunate to be able to save their lives.
>
> They were taken off the ice by Skipper Stephen
> Luther in the schooner *Freda D* and were brought to
> Carbonear. King had on board *Lily Beatrice* the value
> of his winter's work for lumber, sold at St. John's and
> a little money, all of which went down with his
> schooner.

King was taken to St. John's and there his friend from
Carbonear (who remained unidentified) met and took him

to a hotel for breakfast. King hoped some government agency or shipping authority would pay for his passage home for he had lost all his cash and supplies. Up to the time of the shipwreck, Matthais King was an independent businessman, but because of an unfortunate clash with the sea he had been left nearly destitute. The letter writer concluded that there were great odds against Skipper King in the attempt to fight a battle for a little bread and butter.

Today St. Jones Within is a viable picturesque town with a population of about 150.

ANOTHER SHIP FROM MONROE, TRINITY BAY

A generation or two ago, Newfoundlanders could and frequently did make up a song or poem about any event of significance. Much of Newfoundland and Labrador's oral history was and still is preserved in songs, poems and yarns, or stories. The ever-present songwriter must have been at Monroe, Trinity Bay, in the fall of 1916 for the launch of a ship.

Another schooner, the *Douglas Haig*, slid down the ways and, in a burst of pride for Monroe shipbuilders and patriotism for the country, the songwriter recorded the event in a 'verse or two.'

Certainly the lines perpetuate local heros — Stone, Gulliver, Frampton. Owners and managers of the shipyards, Emanuel and Henry Stone, were master shipwrights themselves. Emanuel owned a general business in Monroe. The vessel was designed by George Gulliver and the master shipwright on the site was Josiah Frampton.

Over the years, about forty ships were built at the yards, ranging from the first, the forty-two-ton *Cumberland* launched in 1901, to *Lady MacDonald* and 379-ton *Terra Nova* launched in 1947. One of the three-masted terns built was the 242-ton schooner *Union Jack* (see photo on page 75). Another of the well-known vessels built there was the *Norma and Gladys*, which eventually became a government-owned "showcase" or heritage ship for the province.

The poem "Douglas Haig" also pays tribute to a war champion, British field marshal Douglas Haig, after whom the ship was named. In 1915 Haig became the commander in chief of the British expeditionary force in France and distinguished himself in World War I.

Monroe, lying about twelve miles northward from St. Jones Within "as the crow flies" with the great island of Random between them, has always had a reputation for producing fine schooners.

Douglas Haig didn't last long however and it disappeared during World War I. Its demise wasn't attributed to shoddy workmanship. *Douglas Haig* made a voyage overseas in early January 1917, from St. John's to Alicante, Spain, with salt fish, but had never reported. In 1917 the German navy sea blockade and offensive was in full swing and most people believed the schooner fell a victim to a U-boat.

After the war, examination of German war

DOUGLAS HAIG

Monroe, a place on Trinity Bay
Not known to many men today
Is where last week on the stocks there lay
The fine ship *DOUGLAS HAIG*.

On Tuesday morning at high tide
A bottle broke against her side
And gently forward with a glide
Came this ship *DOUGLAS HAIG*.

She never for an instant stuck
Just took the water like a duck
We wished her all the best of luck
This good ship *DOUGLAS HAIG*.

The biggest ship up to today
That has been launched in Trinity Bay
The finest model you will say
When you see *DOUGLAS HAIG*.

Emanuel and Henry Stone
By enterprise and grit have shown
This country's build will soon be shown
Through ships like *DOUGLAS HAIG*.

It was George Gulliver designed
This finest vessel of her kind
Why go to Canada to find
Such ships as *DOUGLAS HAIG*.

Josiah Frampton built the ship
A man, who has a thorough grip
Of all that's wanted; here's a tip
If you want a *DOUGLAS HAIG*.

The men upon the pay roll sheet
As carpenters you cannot beat
Just as the Germans can't defeat
That other *DOUGLAS HAIG*.

records revealed the fate of the missing schooner. *Douglas Haig* had been intercepted and sunk by an enemy sub on February 1, 1917. All crew was lost: Morgan and Thomas Eavis, Ramea; Alfred Eavis and his brother-in-law, Chester Hickman of Grand Bank; and James Green, residence unknown. Alfred Eavis, who originally belonged to Ramea, was married in Grand Bank and was twenty-six years old. Hickman was a youth of eighteen.

Another Monroe schooner. Built in 1946 by shipwright Henry William Stone of Monroe, the fifty-ton *Cathelia* (above) was initially owned by W & J Moores of Carbonear, but in 1956 Jensen's business of Harbour Breton purchased the banking schooner.

Tom and Hermon Jensen used it as a coasting vessel to bring supplies and as a banker. Three skippers who commanded this vessel were Hermon Jensen, Josiah N. Bullen, and Pius Augot of Harbour Breton. Its fishing crew in August of 1961 is known: from Harbour Breton, Josiah Bullen, engineer John McDonald, cook Lloyd Buglar, and seamen George W. Cox. Seamen or deckhands Thomas Lambert and Richard J. Lambert of Miller's Passage and Theodore Snook, Sagona Island.

In April 1966, Jensen's Limited sold *Cathelia* to Dorman Roberts of Triton. In November 1972 it was destroyed by fire while moored on the north side of Triton. Photo and information courtesy of Doug Wells.

Chapter 28

Finding an Abandoned Schooner

Green's Harbour/Port Union

For many years, Captain Fred Tulk of Port Union skippered the M.V. *Swile*. Before his tenure on the *Swile*, he had charge of another Port Union vessel, *F.P. Union*, named after the Fishermen's Protective Union headquartered in Port Union. On June 11, 1929, Tulk participated in a unique event at sea that many captains never experience in a lifetime — finding an abandoned ship.

Tulk and *F.P. Union* left St. John's at 2 a.m. Tuesday, June 11, with a general cargo for Port Union. By 6:30 a.m. he was in Baccalieu Tickle, a ship's passage between Baccalieu Island and two bays, Conception Bay and Trinity Bay. As dawn broke, the crew saw a schooner with a distress flag in the rigging. Tulk and his crew reckoned its position to be a half mile northwest by west from the Northwest Point of Baccalieu Island.

To their surprise, when they drew close to the schooner, it could be seen that no one was aboard. In fact the decks were strewn with wreckage, sails and riggings and the foremast had been broken off eight feet below the crosstrees. The mainmast head was gone and the anchor chain was out, trailing with the anchor presumably attached to it. The cabin of the schooner was locked, but the forecastle was open. It was evident the schooner had been through a severe storm, but where was the crew? In the cabin? Safe on shore? Lost?

Motor vessel *F.P. Union* in ice. In June 1929, it towed the drifting abandoned schooner *Alice C* into Port Union.

On board *Alice C* was a load of barrel hoops, two or three small fishing boats, two cod traps, and other fishing gear. Presumably the crew was to engage in fishing probably out of St. John's.

Tulk and crew could see the name of the vessel, *Alice C*, but the crew was nowhere to be found. The schooner, about fifty tons, was owned, as they found out later, by Ebenezer Cram of Green's Harbour, Trinity Bay. It had been on a voyage to St. John's under command of Captain Jonathan Rogers of Green's Harbour with his crew of four.

A fishing community located south of Heart's Delight-Islington, Trinity Bay, Green's Harbour has been shown on Newfoundland maps from as far back as 1775. A good supply of trees for timber attracted early settlers when they saw the potential for boat building.

It is likely that Green's Harbour was first settled in the early 1800s by families from southern England, Old Perlican, and Heart's Content. Early settlers were John March, John Day, Jim Green, and William Brace. John Green occupied a fishing room at Green's Harbour in the winter of 1800-1801 and it is possible the harbour was named after him.

Lovell's Newfoundland Directory (1871) also lists family names of Cooper, Day, Harnum, Hopkins, Houch, Matcher, Penny, and Rowe at that time. Early occupations in Green's Harbour were the small boat inshore fishery, the Labrador fishery, small-scale agriculture and, later, logging and saw mill operations. The rise of small, privately-owned saw mills came in the early 1900s and included the Drover mill which sent dressed lumber to St. John's from around 1915 to 1935. Other mill owners included Vernon Taylor, who manufactured fish boxes and butter boxes, and Samuel Cooper, Joseph Green, and George and Charles Harnum.

A small boom in the saw milling industry took place in the 1930s and 1940s, when schooners owned by the Greens, Drovers, Harnums, and Crams were outfitted by St. John's merchants for the lumber trade. Local merchants such as Ebenezer J. Cram, whose business exists in Green's Harbour today, collected fish and wood products and shipped it by schooner to St. John's.

This was the work of *Alice C* as it left Green's Harbour on Monday morning, June 10. While off Red Head Cove, the schooner hit a strong gale and while the crew battled the wind, the masts broke with the mainmast going first. Captain Rogers tried to bring the schooner up with a kedge anchor attached to a line, but this failed and he let go the main anchor to keep the vessel steady.

Another Newfoundland schooner requiring assistance as the *Gladys Mosher* (above) is being towed by the S.S. *Glencoe* in 1928. *Gladys Mosher* was built in Smith and Rhuland yards, Lunenburg in 1917, and was involved with one rescue at sea. On November 24, 1919, a message came to the Minister of Shipping from Albert Haynes of Catalina, saying that the schooner *J.R. Bradley* had been abandoned at sea on November 2. *J.R. Bradley* left Sydney on October 22, laden with coal for Catalina, but sprang a leak. Residents of Catalina had been so long without word from the *Bradley*, they assumed it was lost at sea. However, the crew had been rescued by *Gladys Mosher* and taken to Barbados. Photo courtesy of Doug Burgess, Nova Scotia.

Using the schooner's motor boat, Rogers and his crew then left *Alice C* and went in to Red Head Cove to telegraph the Marine and Fisheries Department. Rogers was hoping for some sort of assistance from a St. John's harbour tug or a coastal steamer. If either of these was in some nearby port perhaps it would take the beleaguered schooner in tow.

While the crew was in Red Head Cove, Tulk and *F.P. Union* found and took the schooner in tow, but not without some minor damage to his own vessel. By the time Captain Rogers again reached the area where he left *Alice C*, it was nowhere to be seen.

Schooner *Millie Ford* (above) tied up at Bloomfield in the palmy days when it was owned by the Parsons' family. Built in Essex, Massachusetts, as the *Hazel R. Hines* in 1904, this seventy-nine net ton banker was sold in 1925 to Captain John C. Ford of Port aux Basques who changed the name to *Millie Ford*, in honour of Captain Ford's mother. The schooner was brought to Newfoundland by the captain, his son Augustus and Wesley Bennett and converted into a coasting schooner designed to carry supplies and coal.

In 1932 Captain Edgar Parsons of Bloomfield, Bonavista Bay, bought the schooner and eventually Captain James Parsons commanded it. When lost it was owned by the Honorable J. (John) W. Pickersgill, a Liberal Member of Parliament in the Pearson era. Photo courtesy of Bruce Neal.

About 12:30 p.m. Tuesday, Tulk arrived in Port Union with the schooner, and it wasn't long before details on the abandoned schooner came in. The same evening, Rogers and his crew steamed into Port Union by motor boat.

Owner Cram came by the steamer *Home* Wednesday afternoon. Cram said neither *Alice C* nor the cargo was insured, but he worked out a deal between himself and the salvors of *Alice C*. Within a day Cram, Captain Rogers, and his crew took their vessel back to Green's Harbour.

Schooner *Millie Ford* wrecked near Cape Race on June 18, 1959. A day later the deckhouse and part of the deck (above) drifted in at Long Beach. Max Kennedy stands on deck. Photo courtesy of Bruce Neal.

Chapter 29

Battle with the Atlantic

The steamer *Florizel* became better known to many present-day Newfoundlanders when author Cassie Brown described its loss in her captivating book *A Winter's Tale*. *Florizel*, the pride of Bowring's Red Cross line, ran aground in February 1918 off Cappahayden and ninety-four passengers and crew lost their lives.

Florizel's regular run was from St. John's to Halifax and New York. In 1914, on one of its trips from New York, the passenger steamer brought a shipwrecked crew home to Newfoundland. Captain Arthur Dean, mate George Bartlett, bosun Joseph Osmond, cook John Forward, seamen Albert Pilgrim, and George Penney, all of Carbonear, had a thrilling epic tale of the sea to relate which ended with a brief stay in New York.

It began on January 8, 1914, when their schooner *Annie E. Banks* left Herring Neck, Notre Dame Bay, for Gibraltar with a cargo of fish. From the beginning, a barrage of winter gales, intense frost, high seas, and heavy snow pounded the schooner. From January 12 to 14 it iced up, forcing Captain Dean to "heave to" under a small sail. Even with its head into the wind, seas occasionally broke across the deck.

Two immense waves broke across the vessel and swept away everything movable — lifeboats, water casks, and deck gear. It tore away the rudder and created general havoc with the crew struggling to keep the ship afloat. When one of the boats went over the side, it crushed Captain Dean's leg as he was attempting to secure the boat. Part of the rudder broke away and damaged the planking, causing a severe leak.

For four days and nights the men, with little rest, drenched with freezing spray and cold, worked like Trojans at the pumps. To lighten the ship they jettisoned 500 quintals of fish, but the water in the hold gradually rose higher and higher. On January 17, the weather moderated a little and that same evening someone sighted a tramp steamer three miles away and headed west.

The crew lost no time getting off a flare, but it seemed as if the steamer paid no attention and continued steaming away until it vanished over the horizon. To the desperate mariners this seemed to be an intentional move by the steamer as if it had noticed the distress signs but decided not to stop. The crew was disheartened and depressed for they felt *Annie E. Banks* would founder at any minute.

For one more night they laboured at the pumps and tried every means to keep the schooner afloat for a few more hours. At dawn a second steamer could be seen and again the weary crew signaled. This time the ship turned down toward them and eventually proved to be the cargo ship *Indrina*, bound from Swansea, Wales, to New York.

Chief Officer White manned a lifeboat with five Chinese sailors and in four hours of dangerous and hard work in high seas, manoeuvred the boat to the side of the sinking Newfoundland schooner. Dean and his crew were by this time in the rigging and each man jumped into the lifeboat which narrowly avoided being smashed by the wallowing schooner.

Captain Dean, the last to leave, doused the cabin with kerosene and lit it. By the time *Annie E. Banks*' crew reached the side of *Indrina* the schooner was a mass of flames. To keep the lifeboat as light as possible, the shipwrecked crew couldn't bring personal possessions or clothes bags with them. On the steamer they were treated well and given some extra clothing.

When they reached New York they waited for the arrival of S.S. *Florizel* and came home on the steamer on February 6, 1914.

The dredge *Priestman* (above in North Sydney, 2002) served in the 1930s to 1970s in Newfoundland and was a common sight dredging harbours.

One early tragedy associated with the old *Priestman* was the death of Joseph Rogers who was killed going on board *Priestman* on January 24, 1939. He was born in Greenspond and resided on Hamilton Street, St. John's. He left a wife, one daughter, and two sons. (*Observer's Weekly* January 24, 1939). Photo courtesy of Conrad Clarke, North Sydney.

Chapter 30

Torpedoed Three Times in Three Weeks

When initial reports came back to St. John's and Carbonear in February 1917, people feared Captain John Hamilton was a victim of war. He had last been seen with others in a lifeboat as they abandoned a steamer that had been attacked by a U-boat.

How he came to be missing is a strange tale of the sea and the unusual experience of Newfoundland seamen being torpedoed three times by the enemy in the space of three weeks.

The story begins with the schooner *Rose Dorothea*, owned by the Campbell & McKay Company of St. John's. Four of *Rose Dorothea*'s crew — Captain W. Bradbury, R. Richardson, R. Wilcox, and J. St. Clare (unfortunately only initials of their first names were available) — arrived in St. John's in March 1917, and related that while en route to Europe with fish, *Rose Dorothea* was sunk by a German submarine without warning.

It left Newfoundland December 31, 1916, with a cargo of fish for Europe and reached Gibraltar in good time. There Captain Bradbury received orders to proceed to Oporto to discharge his cargo. Following discharge, the next move was Cadiz for salt. Between Oporto and Cadiz, *Rose Dorothea* met its end.

On February 16, the schooner rounded Cape St. Vincent off southern Portugal when an enemy submarine surfaced and sent it to the bottom. The crew was left to the mercy of the wind and waves, but the vessel's boat was equal to the occasion. Within a few hours the schooner *Mayola*, also from St. John's and with a cargo of salt fish shipped by Smith Company, came by. Captain John Hamilton of Carbonear with a Nova Scotian crew — with the exception of seaman Keating, a Newfoundlander — gladly took them aboard.

The 119-ton *Mayola*, once owned in Lunenburg, was fifteen miles off Albufiera, Portugal, when, without warning, it was hit by a torpedo. Again the men had to take to the lifeboats. This time in greater haste than with the sinking of *Rose Dorothea*.

After several hours hard rowing, they reached Tagus on the south coast of Portugal. From there they were sent to Lisbon and then to Falmouth, England, in the Bristol Channel.

At Falmouth, the crew of the two sunken ships, *Rose Dorothea* and *Mayola*, secured a passage west to North America on the royal mail packet steamer *Drina*. Aboard were nearly 500 passengers, including many men of different schooners and steamers which had been sunk through enemy action, all en route to North America.

Bristol Channel, about eighty miles long, opens at southwestern England into the Atlantic. Waiting at the mouth was yet another submarine, as part of the German naval blockade of England. At midnight, *Drina* was on the receiving end of a torpedo and this time crew and passengers barely made it into lifeboats.

Within a few weeks, Captain Bradbury of *Rose Dorothea* had been torpedoed three times and it was the second time for Captain John Hamilton of the *Mayola*.

Drina, a 10,000-ton ship, went down quickly. Crew, passengers, men, women and children rushed on deck half clad, but *Drina* sank slowly and they had time to launch several lifeboats. Soon all the ship's company were away in lifeboats. A biting wind and stinging frost pierced the castaways. After several hours adrift at night, a British trawler found the several lifeboats and carried the people to Liverpool.

All other Newfoundland crewmen were accounted for except Captain Hamilton. The lifeboat he was in had not been located although those rescued had last seen him pulling away from the sinking steamer in a lifeboat filled with British passengers.

The story of the three clashes with enemy raiders appeared in the St. John's *Evening Herald* on March 26, 1917, with the heading **Three Times Torpedoed**. The sub-heading however said, "Capt. Hamilton of Mayola Drowned in Bristol Channel." The story went on to name his siblings: brother Michael Hamilton of Carbonear and sisters Mrs. Charles McCarthy and Mrs. Peter Keough.

The Evening Herald, St. John's, Newfoundland, March 26, 1917

THREE TIMES

Torpedoed by Germans

Crew of 'Rose Dorothea' Were on Three Ships Sunk By Huns

Capt. Hamilton of Mayola Drowned in Bristol Channel

This is how *The Evening Herald* of March 26, 1917, reported the unusual tale of Captain Hamilton.

Although the media and his shipmates didn't know it at the time, Captain Hamilton had been rescued and he eventually returned to Carbonear. According to Frank Saunders in his book *Sailing Vessels and Crews of Carbonear*, Captain Hamilton passed away in Carbonear.

During the era when the banking schooner *Madelyn Hebb* (above) fished out of Lunenburg, two Newfoundland sailors employed on it had a close brush with death. On May 15, 1930, Charles Scott and Joseph Clarke of Fortune Bay became separated from the vessel while hauling trawls on Bankquero Quero. For three days and nights they drifted without food or water and were near the end of their endurance when the schooner *St. Clair Theriault* of Pictou, Nova Scotia, found them and took the two castaways aboard.

On November 12, 1953, schooner *Madelyn Hebb* was heading to St. John's when it encountered gale force winds. To ride out the storm, Captain Billy Parsons with only his two sons aboard, headed the ship toward the Redlands in Western Bay harbour, but around 10 p.m. it dragged anchor and drifted toward the cliff.

The captain and his sons left in dory and reached land at Tacker's Cove. Walking toward the first lighted house they saw, they knocked on the door of Mrs. Elizabeth Rose. Young Gordon Smith, a relative of Mrs. Rose, answered the door to find three shipwrecked men asking for help.

They stayed for two or three days, waiting for winds to abate. But in the interim, *Madelyn Hebb* drifted ashore and was totally wrecked at Ambrose's Point.

The seamen booked a passage to St. John's in Clarence Crowley's car, but paid Mrs. Rose fifty dollars for board and lodging.

In this photo *Madelyn Hebb* has a large hole chopped through the starboard side and some items are left on the rocks. A mast or boom floats off the port side. Photo and information courtesy of Dave Morrissey, St. John's.

Prior to the loss of *Rose Dorothea,* Hamilton had also been shipwrecked in December 1916 in the schooner *Fall River.* He and his Carbonear crew of David Murphy, William French, Douglas Nicholl and mate Murphy of St. John's left Campbellton, Notre Dame Bay, for St. John's. En route, a storm blew them off course and into the mid-Atlantic.

In the gale, the schooner was dismasted when the fore rigging broke — some crew barely escaped with their lives when the spars fell on deck. Three days after they were dismasted and with the ship leaking, Hamilton sighted a passing steamer.

Flares attracted the ship which turned out to be the Norwegian steamer *Barbara.* The Norwegian seamen took Hamilton and his crew off the sinking *Fall River.*

That experience paled with the trauma of the submarine attacks. The crew of the *Rose Dorothea* had been attacked by the enemy three times; Hamilton twice, and he had been reported dead by local newspapers.

Chapter 31

The Ghostly Appearance

Spaniard's Bay/Bishop's Cove/Upper Island Cove

One evening in early November 1925, a Spaniard's Bay mother heard a familiar sound — the horn of a small vessel. She listened again, wanting to be sure. Yes, it was the *Bullbird*'s horn. The five men must be arriving at last. She put on the kettle, moved the pot of soup from the back of the stove to the front and prepared the little home for her son. Then the woman donned her warm coat, threw a heavy shawl over her head and shoulders to ward off the cold damp November evening, and walked to the dock to await the *Bullbird*. The crew must be weary from a long journey from the Labrador fishery in a little craft. November was no easy month for beating the northern seas.

Others were there at the waterfront; they had also heard the plaintive cry of the horn. Through the shimmering evening haze, the faint outline of a small boat appeared, but strangely drew no closer to the dock. Some loved ones called out, but the strange sight faded from view. Glad hearts paused. Was it the five men and the *Bullbird* or a token of a lost ship with five young souls aboard? It disappeared from sight, but the people of Spaniard's Bay were sure of what they saw and knew they heard the horn of an approaching craft. But was it an apparition? No, it seemed so real.

Sadly, loved ones and relatives went back home to discuss what they had seen and to prepare others for the worst news. Others comforted the families, but they too knew the meaning of a token, an unearthly representation of a restless soul. Days passed and still no tidings of *Bullbird* and its five occupants.

They were all young except one. Gilbert Lynch of Bishop's Cove and John Strickland, Spaniard's Bay, were both eighteen; Lewis Gosse, Spaniard's Bay, was nineteen. Twenty year old William Lynch belonged to Upper Island Cove and the owner and skipper of *Bullbird*, Harold Smith of Bishop's Cove, was thirty-six.

Family groups met to discuss the possible route that the little craft might have taken and to discuss the sightings of *Bullbird* by other craft. Any talk of possible tidings or its whereabouts would be good news. Why would five people leave the Labrador coast for Conception Bay in a boat as small as that? *Bullbird* was a decked fishing boat with motor engine and sails and had been working hook and line off Horse Harbour, Labrador. It was first thought the seven-ton boat was owned by G. & M. Gosse's business, but it had been built seven years previously by owner Harold Smith. Gosse's firm only provided fishery equipment to Smith.

Owner Harold Smith, a competent and careful man, had taken *Bullbird* to the Labrador fishery the year it was built, came back on another occasion and returned the next spring successfully. Using a series of stops or safe harbours along the route and by watching for fair weather, he could take the boat down again.

It was a twist of fate that two extra men were aboard the *Bullbird*. Lewis Gosse, the son of Martin Gosse, and John Strickland, a worker for Martin Gosse, were slated to come home from the Labrador on G. & M. Gosse's schooner *Harry Smith*. The schooner was wrecked at Emily Harbour in a September storm. Consequently many fishing crews that went north on *Harry Smith* had to return to Conception Bay on the coastal steamer

Meigle. Gosse and Strickland decided not to come by the coastal boat, but booked their passage on *Bullbird*.

Martin Gosse objected to this plan and advised Lewis and John to wait for the *Meigle* and to come home with him and the rest of the fishing crews. But the two boys, filled with a sense of adventure, preferred coming on this motor boat. Even after the two left, Martin sent a boat after them to bring them back, but failed to find them. On his way home on the *Meigle*, Martin sent a message to Battle Harbour for Lewis and John to wait there. The father would make other travel arrangements for them and find a way of leaving *Bullbird* at Battle Harbour.

When Martin Gosse arrived in Spaniard's Bay in late October, he had word *Bullbird* arrived in Seldom-Come-By and immediately sent a telegram warning them not to leave until fair weather. Now his son and his friend and the three others were missing.

At 3 p.m. Wednesday, October 28, *Bullbird* left Seldom in company with the schooner *Scotch Cure* of Wesleyville; both passed the Penguin Islands at 11 p.m. and parted company. This was the last sighting of *Bullbird*. The wind was moderate, but a high sea was running at Cape Freels. Captain Burgess of the steamer *Meigle* thought that the missing craft never made it around Cape Freels. A storm descended on the area the next day.

Captain Edward Murphy of the schooner *Bertha May* went north on the evening of October 28 and rounded the cape before the wind chopped north northwest the next day. If *Bullbird* had sailed safely past treacherous headlands, it would have reached Greenspond by the next day.

On November 20, 1925, the last newspaper posting appeared for the five seamen which said the motor boat *Bullbird* was still missing and that "all hopes are abandoned for its safety." So ended the mystery, but there are those even today who know the story of the mournful wail of a motor boat's horn as the ghostly token of *Bullbird* makes its mysterious rendezvous in Spaniard's Bay.

Chapter 32

In the Wake of the Wop

Port-de-Grave/St. John's/Argentia

I ron ore was first mined at Bell Island in 1895 and with the production of ore came an increased need for goods and services. In 1909, George Neal of St. John's became a vessel owner and began freighting supplies to the people of Bell Island and the mines.

Neal founded the Bell Island Steamship Company and, some time later, his son William R. Neal operated the business. The Bell Island Steamship Company wound up existence in 1992 under the ownership of grandson Bruce Neal. As the company name implies, its ships were not schooners but steamers, generally averaging about 100 tons.

In their time the steamers were dependable and familiar sights around St. John's and Conception Bay, but each eventually succumbed to the hazards of the sea around Newfoundland. For example, the S.S. *Mary*, one of the first steamers owned by the business, was wrecked through an odd accident at Port-de-Grave on November 16, 1929.

Under command of Captain Mark Saunders, the steamer arrived in ballast at Harold Andrews' premises in Port-de-Grave. It tied up next to the wharf to receive a shipment of fish, but because of considerable swell in the harbour, had to back out. A motor boat owned by William John Dawe and Charles Tucker was moored a short distance from the wharf and had a long length of chain or "collar" attached to an anchor. The chain, unseen and unknown by *Mary's* crew, entangled in the propeller and brought it to a stop. Without power, the steamer drifted on the rocks in the high wind and grounded between two boulders; one went through the bottom.

S.S. *Mary* (above) aground near the land wash and fishing stages in Port-de-Grave on November 16-17, 1929. In the background is Ship Cove Point. David and William Neal went to the wreck site by the next day, but there was already three or four feet of water in the hold. Photo courtesy of William A. Neal and Bruce Neal.

S.S. *Mary*, built in 1888 at Grimsby, England, was 104 gross tons. In this photo it lies near a fishing stage belonging to brothers Albert, Abram, and Samuel Dawe in Ship Cove, Port-de-Grave. Although S.S. *Mary* was fifty-nine years old, it had been extensively rebuilt over the years. The year it was lost, 1929, it had all top siding renewed and two years previously had a new boiler installed. Those repairs cost $8,000, but no insurance was carried on S.S. *Mary*. Photo courtesy William A. Neal and Bruce Neal.

S.S. *Mary* was never refloated and for many years its remains could be seen on the bottom in Ship Cove, Port-de-Grave.

S.S. *Mary* (above aground in Port-de-Grave). Managing owner William R. Neal of St. John's had the steamship *Mary* in continuous operation for over twenty years. Other steamships owned by Neal over the years were *Baleine*, *Baronet*, *Euphrates*, *Mary Smith*, *Oban*, *Pawnee*, *W.A. Walker*, *Walter Kennedy*, *Wop*, and *Wren*. Photo courtesy of Mona Petten.

S.S. *H.A. Walker* was built during World War I when the Canadian government had a number of small wooden steamships constructed in Levis, Quebec. Each vessel averaged 100 tons and was eighty-feet long, with two masts equipped with sails, making them, in effect, steam/sail vessels.

Around 1919, Patten and Forsey's business at Grand Bank bought the steamer. *H.A. Walker*, the only vessel powered by steam ever owned in Grand Bank, transported fish and supplies around the South Coast, passengers to and from St. Pierre, and coal from Sydney. When Patten and Forsey's business dissolved in 1922, the steamer was sold to the Bell Island Steamship Company.

H.A. Walker carried goods and passengers to Bell Island and other Conception Bay ports under the command of Captain Llewellyn Carter. On February 17, 1938, the steamship, en route from St. John's to Carbonear and laden with coal, was caught and squeezed by Arctic drift ice about a mile off shore from Pouch Cove. Later that night, ice driven by strong wind punctured the hull of the steamer and it slowly went down. Only ice pressure kept the vessel from submerging completely.

The next night, February 18, Captain Carter and his four crewmen abandoned the doomed *H.A. Walker*, but set it afire. The steamer went to the bottom shortly after.

S.S. *H.A. Walker* (left) and S.S. *Mary Smith* (right) were two steamers owned by Neal's Bell Island Steamship Company of St. John's in the 1930s. Both receive cargo, mostly oil in drums, at George Neal's wharf, St. John's. Note two types of land transportation, a draft horse and cart, right, and a truck, centre, probably with coal in sacks. Photo courtesy of Bruce Neal, St. John's.

About the same time the *Walker* sank off Pouch Cove, its sister ship, the S.S. *Wop*, was in trouble in Placentia Bay. On Wednesday, February 16, 1938, the steamer butted its way through the harbour ice at Argentia and the *Wop* too became stuck. *Wop*, a 100-ton vessel, owned by the Bell Island Steamship Company, was a well-known steamer around the east coast of Newfoundland.

Wop, under the command of Captain Norman, was returning from Placentia Bay ports with a load of herring for the North American Fisheries Plant, a San Francisco-owned operation based at Argentia. It was not Arctic ice floes, as was the case with *H.A. Walker*, but the intense frost of the recent cold spell which had put about six inches of "harbour ice" on the surface that spelled doom for the *Wop*. The little wooden steamer could not make its way to the wharf.

Early Thursday afternoon, the Newfoundland Railway's S.S. *Home*, one of the Alphabet Fleet, steamed into Argentia. *Home*, though one of the smaller members of the fleet, was several times larger than S.S. *Wop*, and had a steel hull. It had little difficulty cutting a channel through the harbour ice. Both ships then berthed to discharge cargoes.

The 1938 blocking of Argentia and other Placentia Bay harbours by harbour ice was noted to be a rare occurrence; unusual enough that wooden ships could not navigate through it. *Wop*'s attempt caused it to leak and a few days after, February 28, the little steamer sank at Merasheen, Placentia Bay, never to be refloated.

The Bell Island Steamship Company had lost several small steamers within a few years: *Mary* at Port-de-Grave, *H.A. Walker* at Pouch Cove, *Wop* at Merasheen and on December 5, 1934, the S.S. *Walter Kennedy* sank at Miquelon Head. In 1916, George Neal purchased the S.S. *Wren*, a North Sea trawler. Three years later it was put on the Labrador service. On September 24, 1924, it loaded freight at Davis Inlet, but struck ledges near Lopside Island and sank.

In addition, the passenger ship S.S. *Pawnee*, which had been replaced by the motor ship *Maneco*, was beached at Harbour Grace where it was broken up.

Chapter 33

Walter Waugh: Castaway of Biscayan Rock

Harbour Main/Biscayan Rock, Cape St. Francis

A t one period in the history of transportation on the Avalon Peninsula, a mail and passenger steam packet ran a regular route from St. John's to Conception Bay ports — Bell Island, Carbonear, Harbour Grace, Brigus, and other ports. Its route went north from St. John's, around Cape St. Francis and then southerly down into Conception Bay. The mail packet left early in the morning for the trip with stops would take the better part of a day.

In 1875, the S.S. *Hercules*, captained by Samuel Blandford, worked the route. Early Tuesday morning November 30, 1875, it steamed out of St. John's. At 12 p.m. as *Hercules* neared Cape St. Francis, the lookout saw a man on one of the Biscayan Rocks waving a red scarf. The Biscayan Rocks are five crags in the ocean, lying a few hundred feet east of Biscayan Cove, Cape St. Francis. From the look of things, the person was barely able to wave or move and looked fatigued and weak from exposure. As *Hercules* closed in, it could be seen it was a man, but how did he end up on this barren crag? Was it a lone fisherman? Was there a shipwreck?

The weather for the end of November was raw and cold. Waves were choppy and a fresh breeze blew. Captain Blandford put *Hercules* in the lee of the rock, lowered his boat and manned it with six of the ablest hands on board.

They carried lines with them and when the lifeboat drew as near the rock as safety would permit, someone threw a rope. After several attempts the rescuers could not get the heavy line within reach.

Biscayan Rocks looking easterly from Cape St. Francis. Walter Waugh was marooned on these crags for several hours before he was rescued. For an ariel view of the scene, see page 163.

The boat returned to *Hercules* to get a lighter line with a fishing jigger attached. Again the boat's crew rowed as close as possible, threw the line and the man caught it. But the force of surf and waves between the boat and rock was so great the line broke and again the boat went back to *Hercules*.

This time the crew located another fishing line together with a life preserving vest; in case they had to drag the man through the surf. While the men in the small boat rowed out, Blandford fired a rocket with a line attached in an attempt to get it over the rock. *Hercules* was to the leeward which meant he was firing into a strong wind and the rocket line missed.

Meanwhile the boat men were making the third attempt to pluck the weary man from the rock. This time they were successful. The castaway secured the life preserver around him, held the line and the rescuers pulled him aboard the lifeboat through the waves and whitecaps breaking near and over Biscayan Rocks. From the time he was first sighted until the rescue, three and a half hours had elapsed.

Once aboard the lifeboat they learned he was Walter Waugh of Harbour Main. Incredibly he had been on the rock, exposed to waves, wind, cold and sleet, since 8 p.m. on Monday — nineteen and a half hours. Waugh had been there sixteen hours without seeing anyone or the sign of a ship, then three and a half more hours as *Hercules*' crew tried to rescue him.

He was not questioned much for it could be seen he was in shock from his frightful experience, cold to the bone and weary from lack of sleep and the loss of energy from clinging to his precarious perch. On board *Hercules*, Blandford fed Waugh warm food and liquids, exchanged wet clothing for dry, and placed him in a warm bed.

Eventually his tale was told. Waugh was part of the crew of the schooner *Hopewell* of Harbour Main, skippered by a Captain Joy. (The papers of the day spelled his name as such, but this may be the Wall surname.) Owned by merchant Robert Grieve of St. John's, the schooner was built in Green Bay in 1861.

Hopewell left St. John's for Harbour Main at 4 p.m. Monday, November 29, 1875, with a cargo of provisions. In the evening, the weather came in dirty with rain and sleet. In the course of rounding Cape St. Francis, the ship struck the Biscayan Rocks and immediately broke to pieces. Of the eight aboard, only Walter Waugh reached the relatively safety of one islet; he had not seen what happened to the others, but assumed they were swallowed up by the sea. Not much of the crew's identity is known except there were three brothers named Joy aboard, all of Harbour Main. They were sons of William Joy who is said to have died of a broken heart on February 25, 1876, not long after the mishap.

On Wednesday, December 1, Captain Blandford landed Waugh at Brigus where he found transportation to
Harbour Main. At home he related the tragic story of what
happened to *Hopewell* and how he alone, through some
unknown store of determination and strength, was saved
on the Biscayan Rocks.

Chapter 34

Four Hours on Anvil Rock

Pouch Cove/Carbonear

> *My father and I reefed the mainsail; my brother and the other man reefed the foresail. I said to my father, "I don't see any hope here." He said, "No my boy! I don't either."*
>
> Henry Charles Snow
> Nightfall, November 10, 1890

Those prophetic words were spoken just northeast of Pouch Cove at a rather unknown crag called Anvil Rock. Anvil Rock and Anvil Head are situated east of Biscayan Cove between Cape St. Francis and Pouch Cove on the Avalon Peninsula (See photo on page 155). Many years ago Biscayan Cove was a small but viable fishing community. To the surprise of the people in the cove, one wild and stormy evening they found a young man clinging to Anvil Rock for dear life.

The story of the man and his desperate fight for life begins in St. John's on November 9, 1890, and is best told by the survivor himself, Henry Charles Snow of Bay Roberts.

Sailing together with about twenty other vessels, the little eighteen-ton *Daisey Mae* left St. John's with supplies. Most of the little ships headed for various points along Conception or Trinity Bay; the *Daisey Mae* was en route to Bay Roberts. It had four crew: the captain and owner Charles Snow, his two sons, James, age twenty-eight, seventeen year old Henry Charles Snow, and another hired man. Also making the trip was the captain's thirty-two year old wife Melina (Heirlihy) Snow. She was his second wife and a step-mother to Henry Charles and James.

In the evening of November 9, a favourable wind filled the sails and many vessels rounded Cape St. Francis including *Daisey Mae*. Henry Charles remembered that the wind chopped from the west, blowing very strong and the schooner returned to St. John's:

> We left again the next morning, November 10. We reached across the Bay towards the North Shore, but as the wind was very heavy we had to run back. Then my father said we could go into Biscayan Cove. Darkness and wind came on, but we kept watch. We then reefed our sails when a strong wind and sea chopped. My father and I reefed the mainsail; my brother and the other man reefed the foresail.
>
> I said to my father, "I don't see any hope here."
>
> He said, "No my boy! I don't either."
>
> Just as these words were spoken the chain broke and instead of drifting out to sea we were cast in on the shore. I ran forward to see where we were going, but saw nothing ahead only death and the cliff.
>
> I called to my brother James to get the dory for that was the only chance we had of being saved. We weren't long putting the dory overboard. I ran to the cabin and called to my step-mother to come as quickly as she could.
>
> I went for the dory pretty lively, and jumped in. The tackles (ropes) were in the dory. My brother was in the after part; the other man was in the forward part of the dory. I then held on with my hands and the rail of the vessel with my toes in the risings of the dory.
>
> I found it very hard to hold on when the vessel would swing in and out with the sea. I was some time

like that waiting for my father to come. There were three seas that almost filled the dory.

Father was on deck by the companionway and we didn't think there was anything wrong with him. We should have moved the dory down to the after part of the vessel and took him aboard. The last sea came and I saw my father walk forward.

As he passed by I said, "Father, pull me in."

He said, "I can't, my boy," and he passed on.

I knew then and there was something wrong with him. I managed to get in on the deck of the schooner myself and as I let go the dory, the seas drove it under the bow of the vessel. On my way forward I was knocked down.

Against the foremast I saw someone fast to the rigging. I got alongside and caught him hold; it was my brother.

He said, "Pull me in as fast as you can."

I pulled my brother in and I never saw him alive again. He must have been killed when the mast went overboard.

After I pulled my brother in I went forward to get the other man. He had caught hold to the jib stay. I did my best to get him on board the dory, but the bowsprit took against the cliff and caught me between the bulwarks. I stood to my feet again.

I said, "I got to leave you my poor fellow and try to do the best I can for myself."

I looked on the lee side and could see somebody against the rigging. I walked down alongside him and it was my father. At the time it was very dark. Father told me to jump.

I said, "Father, hold on till I see."

He let go the rigging and held the tackle that was against the fore rigging. He said no more to me. I caught the rigging with both hands. I could not tell where I was going to jump — it was only by chance — as I pitched on my feet the sea threw me on the top of what is called the Anvil Rock.

Henry Charles Snow didn't know at that time who or what surrounded him, if anyone had seen the wreck, or if he would ever reach land. He couldn't get to the dory nor get back aboard *Daisey Mae*, now breaking up in as it pounded against the cliff. Undoubtedly the crew, his father, brother and the sailor, had drowned or were killed by pounding debris. His step-mother, when he last saw her, was in the dory near the side of the wreckage. He was on Anvil Rock near Biscayan Cove, close to land yet a narrow stretch of boiling surf separated the rock from a mass of stone, Anvil Head.

Biscayan Cove, a rugged cove with a landing place barely suitable for a small boat, had settlers as early as 1612. Prime fishing grounds were once located off the cove and fishing/farming families like Baldwin, Bragg, Butt, Connors, Diamond, Evans, Hudson, Legrow, Moulton, and Moores prospered there. In 1935, seventy-four people lived in Biscayan Cove, but many moved to Pouch Cove or St. John's and no one lives there today.

But on that dark night of November 10, from the top of narrow Anvil Rock, young Snow saw no one. All he could see was "a gulch between me and the mainland."

> I crawled to the back of the rock, looking for places to hold on to. I used to watch the seas when they would pass over me and I would beat my hand and feet to keep life in myself. I wondered if I would live until daylight.
>
> It was four long lonely hours I spent there, hearing nothing only the sea, barrels and lumber dashing against the cliff, and the cries of my poor step-mother was the hardest of all.
>
> I did my best to look about to see if I could see or hear anyone from the shore. At last I saw a small light. I yelled out with all my might and I heard a man say to another, "There's a man on the shore, wherever he is."
>
> I yelled three times more and they came pretty straight for me. They came on the edge of the cliff,

and all they could see was my white face. They asked me who was with me, and I said, "As far as I knew, the others were drowned."

I asked them to try and get me off the rock and quick. Some of the men went back to the lighthouse to get a lifeline and torches. Three men stayed on the cliff. As each sea would pass over me, they would call out and ask if I was all right. I would answer back, "Yes."

They would tell me to hold on. By and by they made a big fire on the cliff and could see me all plain then. One man got down as close as he could and he had a jigger and line.

"Look out!" he told me and I said, "All right."

The first throw of the line the jigger caught in the sleeve of my coat. I tied the line around my waist and called out to the men to take in the slack.

The sea was running very high in the gulch. They pulled me gently across and up over the cliff. When they got me, they were very glad. And you may think I was glad too after so long wet, cold, and hungry. They took me to a comfortable home where I was well-cared for.

After they saw I was all right, they went down to the cove where the wreck was. They found my stepmother, floating in the sea. She was the first they got out and they trawled all that week until they found the other three bodies. I came home to Bay Roberts with the other three corpses for their burial.

Henry Charles Snow concludes his horrific tale in a note of gratitude for the men of Biscayan Cove and Pouch Cove who had done all they could to rescue and then comfort him. His father, Charles Snow, had planned to buy a newer and larger schooner and had made every sacrifice to improve his business position in Bay Roberts.

As a footnote to this marine disaster, James Snow, who drowned in the wreck, was married and had a young son, James. James the younger followed the calling of his forebears and became a captain of several vessels, including one of his last commands, the old *Northern Ranger*.

Ariel view of Cape St. Francis, the now abandoned town of Biscayan Cove, and Biscayan Rocks. Also shown are Anvil Head and Anvil Rock. A narrow deep chasm separates the two. This is where Henry Charles Snow was cast by the waves after the wreck of the schooner *Daisey Mae*. Photo courtesy Department of Natural Resources, Surveys and Mapping Division, St. John's.

Chapter 35

Help Arrives on the Cliffs of Horrid Gulch

Cupids/Brigus/Pouch Cove

It was getting late on a Monday night when Eli Langmead, who lived at the north end of Pouch Cove, heard an unfamiliar noise. Someone was shouting and knocking on his door. Langmead had finished his day's work, but he lit his lamp, put on his shirt and opened the door. Three strangers — wet, cold, and nearly exhausted, stood there. As soon as they were able, the men identified themselves as Captain Samuel Spracklin and two crew of the schooner *Waterwitch* of Cupids. It left St. John's earlier that day, November 29, 1875.

Langmead soon learned the news that the vessel had gone ashore in a nearby cove and a number of the people aboard had already perished; others still clung to the rocks in the gulch. Spracklin said the people lost and those still alive and stranded at the base of a cliff belonged to Cupids and Brigus.

Langmead ushered the dazed and weary men into his house, made them comfortable and immediately walked up into the town, calling on the adults in various houses as he went and telling them what had happened.

Pouch Cove, located near the tip of the Avalon Peninsula at Cape St. Francis, had seen several sea dramas played out in that area over the years. In the voyages to and from St. John's and the well-populated bays to the northwest, scores of sailing ships passed near the Cape

St. Francis headlands. Traders were especially busy in the fall. With the high volume of sea traffic came the inevitable shipwreck. One of the most memorable was the loss of *Waterwitch*, a Trinity Bay-built schooner of sixty-two tons with an overall length of sixty-nine feet.

When the news of the *Waterwitch* wreck reached Pouch Cove, most able-bodied men on the north side of the town prepared to go to the scene of the disaster. Some fishermen left by boat, others by land.

The Pouch Cove men figured the wreck had happened at Horrid Gulch, a narrow and treacherous gulch less than a mile and a half northeast of Pouch Cove. It was well-named for the water was deep right to the foot of nearly perpendicular cliffs.

At the north side of the gulch, rock runs almost straight up to the height of over 400 feet. Against this granite face, the sea pounds with tremendous force. On the other side, a narrow ledge ran close to the water's edge.

When the *Waterwitch* struck the cliff, the captain, one of his sons and two other men jumped on a ledge. Other people on board somehow reached ledges on the opposite side, the north face of Horrid Gulch.

George Thomas Noseworthy, one of those saved, described the ordeal afterwards, saying:

> When *Waterwitch* came in the gulch and its quarter neared the rock, Henry Spracklin and I jumped on it. The vessel went out again, and I think about twenty minutes after, it came close again. William Wells, Thomas Ivany, Samuel Row, William Spracklin, and Thomas Spracklin jumped safely.
>
> We were not there very long before the craft smashed up. We heard no cries from those on board. All night it was thick with the exception of one hour when it cleared. We knew the skipper and some others were on the other side of the gulch. We shouted and they shouted back to us. We heard them say they

could climb the cliff if it was daylight and we begged them to try at once.

When the help came we knew it, for we heard strange voices. We kept shouting all night. The spray dashed over us constantly and every twenty minutes or so a large sea would come and dash right over us. I was almost gone once. We had to crouch and cling close together when we saw the sea coming.

George Thomas Noseworthy, one of the *Waterwitch* survivors, held on for hours flat on his stomach on a ledge at the base of the steepest face of the gulch. He could only pray for help; there was nothing else he could do.

Then, between 1 and 2 a.m., rescuers began to arrive at the other side, the less dangerous cliff face where Captain Spracklin and his group had reached.

When Captain Spracklin scaled the cliff he asked his son, Samuel Percy, to remain behind on the ledge. Samuel said he felt strong and in good spirits and his father asked him to stay and talk to and bolster the spirits of those, including Noseworthy, trapped on the steepest side of Horrid Gulch.

The rescuers got into position. Three Pouch Cove men — Robert Moulton and Thomas and Adam Noseworthy — stayed on the less dangerous side, giving assurances to the captain's son below and shouting encouragement to those on the far side. At this time without proper ropes they were powerless to help.

Meanwhile, on the far side, a group of men had gathered, discussing plans to rescue those trapped below. The only way possible was to lower a man over the cliff by a rope in order to determine the location and position of the shipwrecked people.

Alfred Moores of Pouch Cove volunteered for this dangerous work and accordingly had a strong rope fastened around him. He was lowered over the precipice by David Baldwin, Eli Langmead, Christopher Munday, and William Noseworthy. (Ironically one man clinging to the ledge below was a Noseworthy, but the rescuers didn't know that at the time.)

William Langmead was at the end of the rope which was half hitched around a tree for extra security. As the lowering over the cliff progressed, Baldwin, Munday, and the others stationed themselves at various levels between Moores and the top of the cliff ready to provide assistance to him or to any person he might bring up. Others like James, James, Jr., and Uriah Langmead, William Ryan, William Gould, Nathaniel Williams, and John Sullivan were at the top of the cliff waiting to escort the survivors to safety.

One of the people at the scene later wrote about what happened. He identi-

> THOSE LOST ON *WATERWITCH*:
> ALL BELONGED TO CUPIDS OR BRIGUS
>
> Moses Spracklin, son of Capt, 26
> Jonathan Spracklin, 32
> William Spracklin
> Samuel Wells
> Richard Wells
> Elias Ford
> George Ivany
> Solomon Taylor
> Joanna Croke
> Elizabeth Ann Spracklin, 23
> Patience Spracklin
> Malvania Spracklin, 22 (Misidentified in local papers as Amelia or Marlenah Spracklin)
>
> THOSE SAVED ON *WATERWITCH*
> Capt. Samuel Spracklin, aged 50
> Henry W. Spracklin, 43
> Samuel Percy Spracklin, 24
> Thomas Spracklin, 25
> William E. Spracklin, 29
> Richard Ford
> Henry Ivany
> Thomas Ivany
> George Thomas Noseworthy
> Samuel Row
> George Wells
> James H. Wells
> William Wells

fied himself only as G.J.B. (believed to be a Bowring) and said in the St. John's newspaper *The Courier* of December 4, 1875:

> To get any idea of the pluck of these rescuers you must picture to yourself their position on that bleak hillside in the darkness and the cold, clinging for dear life to a rope, the length of which from the top to where Alfred Moores stood at the base of the cliff with the end around his body was eighty-five fathom (510 feet).

On the fourth attempt to the bottom of the cliff, Moores — half swinging, half sliding — went along a steep crevice to a spot over the heads of the survivors.

He could now barely see their faces in the early light of dawn, Tuesday morning. Eight pitiful creatures huddled as close together as they could lie — not standing, but clinging to rock as best they could manage and with all the power they possessed.

Moores, about sixty feet further up, twice threw down a hand rope he had with him, and twice he pulled it back, having missed the spot. The third time with a prayer, "In the Name of God. . ." someone below caught the rope.

Again in *The Courier*, G.J.B. described the final part of the rescue at Horrid Gulch:

> Moores handed down a stronger rope which was made fast around the body of one of the men and he was hauled up to where Moores stood. There this rope was untied and the survivor helped along by the rope held by those, like Langmead, up the cliff face.
>
> In this way all reached the top in safety and the skills and courage of their rescuers were rewarded by success.
>
> But not all were yet safe. One poor young fellow, Percy Spracklin the captain's son, was on a ledge by himself. He, being in the least danger, was left till last. He was there alone, hundreds of feet from his companions, half-dressed, no cap and only one boot. In time rescuers flung a rope to him and he had enough strength left to fasten it around his body and the final survivor of *Waterwitch* was pulled in.

The survivors were taken into Pouch Cove homes for the utmost care. There was no shortage of care givers — in fact the people argued with each other as to who would take them in. Twelve of twenty-five aboard *Waterwitch* drowned, including four women. Three survivors scaled the cliffs. Alfred Moores and his team plucked ten from Horrid Gulch.

The Reverend Reginald M. Johnson, Pouch Cove's Church of England minister, described the rescue saying,

> . . .I was on the spot soon after the terrible news reached the houses and helped to haul up the survivors. Every man was hauled up fast to about 100 fathoms of line. We could hear their cries below us all night. It was frightful. The people here in Pouch Cove behaved nobly.

On that night twelve people perished. When Captain Spracklin walked along the trails to the homes in Pouch Cove, he must have been in a state of shock for in an instant he had not only lost his ship and its supplies, but also his son, a nephew, two daughters-in-law and several close relatives. All four women aboard drowned. One, Elizabeth Ann (Wells) Spracklin at age twenty-three, was a mother of two; four year old Charlotte Ann and Jessie, only eighteen months old. Her husband Samuel Percy Spracklin survived. Widows and relatives of those left behind would, without a breadwinner, no income nor insurance, faced devastating hardships.

Another heartrending case was the death of Elias Ford. His wife, Mary Charlotte (Sprackin), was left, at age forty-nine, with six children, plus she gave birth to the seventh child shortly after the disaster.

As for the heroic men who scaled the cliffs of Horrid Gulch, they were satisfied they had done all they could for the survivors. Alfred Moores later received a silver medal from the Royal Humane Society in England. St. John's citizens presented him with a silver watch. The other Pouch Cove rescuers were awarded bronze medals.

On August 11, 1978, a plaque outlining the *Waterwitch* wreck and commemorating the courage of the rescuers was erected on the public highway at Pouch Cove. The plaque marks the beginning of a trail to Horrid Gulch where a determined group of people helped save several lives many years ago.

Author's note: One of the last items added to *Wind and Wave* was correspondence from Richard Spracklin of Edmonton, the great great-grandson of survivor Thomas Spracklin. He had details on several relatives including the correct identification of the women. According to Richard, all bodies were recovered but one, and the headstones of two of the wives lost on *Waterwitch* are located in the Cupids United Church Cemetery. The folksong "The Waterwitch" says one women was rescued, but newspaper accounts of the day claim that all the women perished.

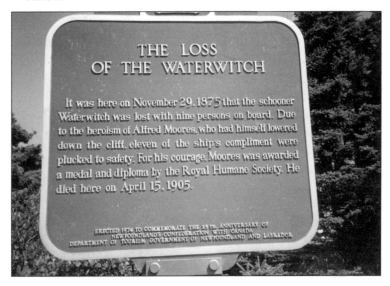

The sign and plaque at Pouch Cove showing the trail to Horrid Gulch. There the rescue of many of *Waterwitch*'s crew and passengers took place. Some discrepancies are noted in the number lost and saved as listed in local archives and the numbers given on the plaque above.

Chapter 36

Collision off Sugarloaf

There is a shipwreck map which shows the numerous shipwrecks that had occurred in the approaches to St. John's harbour. One of the most frequent dates recorded is the 1920s and this is to be expected. In that era hundreds of sailing craft from all over Newfoundland visited St. John's to discharge fish, lumber, vegetables, minerals and a myriad of other products. Schooners departing the hub carried food and supplies to scores of outports in rural Newfoundland.

Accidents were frequent; many had casualties. One relatively obscure incident happened during the night of May 27, 1929. It was a Monday night about 11 p.m. when two small ships neared each other off Sugarloaf. One of the captains was Thomas White of the *Vernie May*, a seventy-six-ton schooner from Herring Neck. *Vernie May*, owned by G.J. Carter, was sailing toward St. John's with a load of limestone from Cobbs Arm. Captain White had four crew.

White was just putting his schooner "in the stays" (changing from one tack to another) when he saw the lights of another vessel approaching and noted:

> While *Vernie May* was actually in the stays, another schooner, the *Emblem of Hope* of forty-six tons, owned and captained by William B. Blackmore and his crew of four and bound from St. John's to Port

> Union, crashed into my schooner on the port side. It
> cut *Vernie May* in half.

The crew of *Vernie May* scrambled from their sinking craft on board the *Emblem of Hope*. They weren't on the deck long when they met a similar predicament. *Emblem of Hope* was also sinking fast from the impact and went down so quickly that the lifeboat floated over the railing. But not before ten men — five from each crew — had climbed aboard.

Emblem of Hope, laden with salt and supplies for Port Union, sank a few minutes after *Vernie May* which went to the bottom like the stone it was carrying. The two crews rowed toward St. John's hugging the shoreline as they went. They reached the harbour about 3 a.m.

Vernie May was not insured, while the other schooner was covered under the Bowring-Job-Monroe-Murray insurance plan. Ironically, *Emblem of Hope* had been formerly owned by G.J. Carter who recently sold the schooner to Captain Blackmore.

* * *

Four years later the S.S. *Sevastapol* became a victim of the Brandies, off Cape St. Francis. In the early 1930s, the Job Brothers purchased the trawler *Sevastapol* owned by the Newfoundland Government; Jobs converted the 2,160-ton trawler into a refrigerated unit specifically to carry frozen fish and blueberries to mainland ports.

At twelve midnight on September 15, 1933, *Sevastapol* left St. John's for Conception Harbour to load blueberries from another vessel, the S. S. *Blue Peter*. *Sevastapol* would then return to St. John's and the cargo would be re-loaded onto S.S. *Fort St. George* which would proceed to New York via Halifax.

At 2:30 a.m. *Sevastapol* struck the Brandies off Cape St. Francis. Captain Ken Barbour, who was asleep at the time of the impact, went to the bridge and ordered full steam astern. The vessel backed off, but filled with water, rolled over, and sank within five minutes.

Barbour and his eight crew managed to float a dory off deck before the steamer sank; the lifeboat and motor boat went down with the ship. The crew rowed into Pouch Cove.

Chapter 37

Beginning and Ending in Nova Scotia

For a few years after the Great War, exports of salt fish to Europe increased and to help transport the product, many Newfoundland businesses purchased tern schooners or three masted schooners — often called foreign-going vessels — from Nova Scotia. Most came from the productive shipbuilding yards in or near Lunenburg, Shelburne, and Lockeport/Allandale. A few were built in other Nova Scotian shipyards; only one Newfoundland tern, *Phileen*, was built in Dartmouth.

Phileen slid down a Dartmouth slipway in 1917; it was 112 feet long and thirty feet wide and netted 265 tons. Owned by the Labrador Export Company, a business based in St. John's, this tern didn't last long in the export trade. Two years after its launch, *Phileen* was abandoned at sea and the crew was landed at Yarmouth, Nova Scotia.

On its final voyage, *Phileen* had eight crew, all Newfoundlanders: Captain Sydney Kendrick, mate Fred Collinby, cook Edward Wakeham, bosun Samuel Parrott, seamen Leo Tobin, Ralph Buckler, Handley Parrott, and Fred Lagrath. This last name may be misspelled in the ship roster and could be McGrath. Sydney Kendrick's father was Captain John Kendrick of

St. John's. Both men were on the schooner *Rose M* when it sank near the Azores in 1922.

On May 6, 1919, *Phileen* left St. John's for Oporto, Portugal, with a full cargo of dry fish and was only out a few days when a storm of wind fell full force upon the Atlantic. The intense wind storm lasted several days and during this period the schooner laboured and strained.

When the storm reached its apex, *Phileen* began to leak. All crew manned the pumps and for five days and nights they worked without letup. It was useless. On May 15, with water steadily gaining and the vessel practically awash in heavy seas, Captain Kendrick decided to abandon ship.

It was only in extreme circumstances that a crew would step into a small lifeboat in mid-Atlantic during a storm, but the fear the ship would sink beneath them forced this drastic step. There was no rescue ship in sight. *Phileen* sank at latitude 39.40 North and longitude 34 West.

For four days and nights, the crew rowed and finally reached "the Western Islands" as the land mass was termed by Newfoundland seamen. This was the Azores, a group of islands lying in the middle of the Atlantic Ocean, about 900 miles west of Portugal. Kendrick and his crew landed at the Isle of Corvo in the northwest part. The men were completely exhausted from nine days and nights of intense labour, keeping the ship afloat and then rowing to land.

Eventually *Phileen*'s crew found a passage to New York where the British Consul arranged for transportation to Yarmouth, Nova Scotia, and there to Halifax and Newfoundland. It was now July 7 and two months had passed since they left on their voyage from Newfoundland for Oporto.

ANOTHER SHIP DISAPPEARS

THE EVENING HERALD,

THE FALCON'S FATE.

Some Reasons Why She Should Not be Given up.—Her Captain a Cautious Man.—He Takes no Chances Which can be Avoided:—His Officers are Like Him.—A Lucky Ship.

The St. John's paper *Evening Herald* of November 14, 1894, says the town was not ready to "give up" hope for the safety of S.S. *Falcon*.

On October 3, 1894, the St. John's ship S.S. *Falcon* left Philadelphia laden with coal for Newfoundland. Bowring Brothers of St. John's owned *Falcon* and Captain H. (Harry) B.J. Bartlett, a master mariner, commanded the ship and his fifteen crew. Captain Bartlett was the youngest son of Captain Abraham Bartlett of Brigus.

By late October the steamer had not reported nor had it been sighted by any other vessel. *Falcon* is listed as **Missing without a Trace** and, as recorded in church records, the place of interment of the crew is given as "The Sea."

S.S. *Falcon* in St. John's harbour. In July 1891 while entering St. John's Narrows, *Falcon* ran down a twenty-ton schooner owned by Stephen Johnson of Northern Bay. There was no loss of life. Photo courtesy of Steve Whitten via Bruce Neal, St. John's.

CREW OF THE MISSING S.S. *FALCON*, OCTOBER 1894

Captain H.B.J. Bartlett, 36, and seaman John Cassidy, 23, both of Brigus; first officer Edward Tracey, 49; second officer Thomas Snow, 33; cook Lawrence Hackett, 42; assistant cook Bernard Wall, 22; fireman John Wall, 50; fireman George Kennedy, 28; second engineer Charles Rankin, 26, all of St. John's; seaman James Burgess, 36, Greenspond; seaman Michael Walsh, 30, Catalina; seaman Stephen Johnson, 30, Seldom-Come-By; seaman John Verge, 25, Old Bonaventure; chief engineer Carl Fischer, 46, Germany; fireman David Barry, 47, Ireland; and seaman E. John Butters, 38, England.

Chapter 38

The Strange Fate of Aureola's Crew

I n the annals of strange Newfoundland sea stories and traumatic losses at sea, the ultimate fate of *Aureola*'s crew must be one of the hardest to fathom. Not only did they fight to survive for three weeks in an epic battle with the sea, but in the end their names were not recorded for posterity.

We may have never known their story but for a newspaper article originating out of Glasgow, Scotland, where the crew had been taken after their rescue. The newspaper interviewed the captain and sent the tale back to Newfoundland. It started and ended when a story came to St. John's in early February 1912, from the Glasgow *Daily Record* that the crew of the barquentine *Aureola* had arrived in Glasgow via London, England. Some wise reporter in Glasgow thought the arduous experience of several Newfoundland sailors on the wild Atlantic was worth a column in a local paper.

When that same column was sent to St. John's in February many people read it with a collective sign of relief — short-lived relief as it turned out for owners Bishop and Sons of St. John's, loved ones and relatives of Captain Christopher Olsen, his nine crew and a young passenger, eleven-year-old Michael McKinley. No word, no news, no report had been received from *Aureola* for nearly two months. All had assumed the ship had been swallowed by one of those frequent mid-winter storms.

The 280-ton barquentine, built at Bradford, England, in 1873, left Troon, Scotland, with coal for St. John's on November 22, 1911. When he described the *Aureola's* final voyage, the Scottish reporter said that "few seamen had ever endured greater hardship than did the crew and passenger of the ill-fated *Aureola* . . . the story of the terrible experiences forms a striking example of the dangers and privations which are so often the lot of those who follow the sea."

But the tale of misery is best told by the captain himself, Christopher Olsen, through the report from Scotland:

> We left Troon and had a fine start. On November 27, 1911, a gale from the northwest came up and increased in velocity for the next twenty-six hours. When the storm was at its height, our mainsail and main staysail, which were new and made in Glasgow of the best canvas, were split. We got these repaired as best we could, but the storm increased and the fury of the wind carried away part of the foresail on December 12.

Olsen's crew patched up the foresail. During the next few days the storm increased such that, on December 20, it was impossible to set an inch of canvas on the ship and Olsen and his crew were forced to lay-to on a starboard tack. Huge seas broke over the decks and *Aureola* was practically under water for a day and a half. As Olsen points out:

> On the afternoon of the following day, a heavy sea, reaching under the double reefs and lower topsail, struck me and knocked me to the deck like a nine-pin. Fortunately I managed to grasp the mizzen sheet and so saved myself from being washed overboard. I felt sick and suffered much pain, my right side being severely injured.

At 8 p.m. a tremendous sea was running and we had to heave to. At midnight the fury of the gale was frightful. The vessel laboured and strained and it seemed impossible that it could live in such a tremendous sea. The waves were running mountains high.

I have had thirty-eight years experience — I was a lad of fifteen when I went on my first voyage — but I never saw anything to equal this. For the next four days to December 25, we encountered gale after gale almost intermittently.

Here in his story to the Scottish papers, Olsen paused to consult his entry in *Aureola*'s logbook. On Friday, January 5, he said, the ship's position became critical as it was labouring heavily. At 4 a.m., in what Olsen termed "a strong, confused sea," *Aureola* shipped a enormous wave. It carried away all the starboard side — stanchions, bulwarks, rails, backstays, and lifeboats. He continued:

We had now sprung a leak and knew we were in the worst plights. The crew worked well, keeping continuously at the pumps. We were to suffer still further, however, from the rage of the tempest.

On January 9, there was another gigantic gale from the southwest. At 1 a.m. we shipped another heavy sea which swept the decks clean. Everything moveable and lashed down went overboard. We were now a total wreck.

Desperately and persistently the men kept pumping, one pump gang relieving the other every two hours. The next day we started to lighten the ship, throwing large quantities of coal overboard. To add to our already desperate condition, the cargo had shifted and to relieve the vessel, we deemed it expedient to cut away the masts and this was done at great peril to the crew on account of the falling wreckage.

Captain Olsen then described the sea and the first sighting of potential rescue ships to the Scottish reporter:

. . .the appearance of the ocean was terrible and the
sound of the gale struck terror to the ear. Still the crew
stuck manfully and silently to the pumps.

He says that they had sighted several other vessels,
made the usual signals of distress, but "Incredibly, not
one — and there were no fewer than five sighted — came
to rescue us from what seemed certain death in the middle of the Atlantic." Olson finished saying,

There was no doubt they had seen us. We were so
close to one vessel that I could see men on her bridge,
but they left us, a helpless wreck in the surging waste
of waters.

For days we managed to keep afloat and on
January 27 we sighted another vessel. It saw our sig-
nals and came alongside. It turned out to be the
Norwegian steamer *Marie* from St. Michael to
London with a cargo of fruit.

With difficulty, the *Marie* lowered its boats and
somehow made two trips to get us all safely aboard.
In our wrecked condition we had kept afloat through
the storm for eighteen days.

Before leaving *Aureola*, we considered it our
duty to set the ship on fire so that, in its wrecked and
submerged state, it would be no danger to navigation.

Captain Christopher Olsen, his nine crew and passenger (although nowhere in his narrative does Olsen say why
young McKinley was aboard) were plucked off a sinking
ship just when death seemed imminent. As they left the
burning *Aureola* behind they would see the glow from the
fire that consumed it from twenty miles away. Olsen says
that Captain Monson and his crew treated them well and
they were taken to the Sailor's Home in London. Olsen
concluded his tale to the Scottish reporter: "It was a terrible experience and I hope I never have to face the same
again."

At this point the narrative from Scotland ends. On February 5, 1912, word reached St. John's that *Aureola* had been abandoned in mid-ocean and its crew was in London, England.

Now they had to get back home. As for the conclusion to this tale, there are no hard facts to describe the tragic ending. Apparently *Aureola*'s crew knew the St. John's steamer *Erna* was being readied for its voyage from Greenock, Scotland, to Newfoundland. It is possible *Aureola*'s sailors figured the 3,000-ton *Erna* would be a much safer and more pleasant voyage than what they had just gone through.

Erna, recently refitted, had been purchased by Captain Linklater who intended to use it in the Newfoundland seal fishery. He was not going to the seal hunt himself, but had hired Captain Jacob Winsor of Wesleyville for that purpose.

Erna left Scotland for St. John's on February 26, 1912, with fifty-one people aboard: its own crew, including Thomas Linklater, his wife and child, Captain Winsor, plus several passengers. As a tragic and final footnote of marine history, it is to be noted *Erna* also carried the eleven rescued souls from *Aureola*. *Erna* never made its destination and to this day is posted as "Missing at Sea."

While local papers list the crew of the S.S. *Erna*, no mention, other than that of Captain Olsen and young McKinley, is made of who *Aureola*'s sailors were.

Chapter 39

S.S. Beverley Disappears

In May of 2002, I searched for details on the disappearance of the S.S. *Beverley*, a steamer which left Harbour Grace on January 23, 1918, for Europe. It had never reported and is listed as "Lost with Crew" although few newspapers of its day carried any details of its possible whereabouts, loss or even speculation of what had happened.

Crewed by twenty-four men, the *Beverley* was 233 feet long, fifty-five feet wide and twenty-two feet deep. Munn and Company of St. John's purchased the steamer from Fearn's shipping business at Placentia. When it arrived in Newfoundland, the deck house — a large passenger accommodation — was removed and this structure, suitable for a restaurant or small motel, was purchased by John J. Duff of St. John's.

On October 30, 1918, a little over nine months after *Beverley*'s disappearance, the inquiry into its loss began. It was chaired by Charles Edward Hunt with lawyer William R. Howley, K.C., representing the owner, W.C. Munn. The inquiry concluded in late January 1919. Several witnesses were called to the stand.

In his statement, George C. Fearn, owner of the shipbuilding yards at Placentia, said he purchased *Beverley* in 1917 from a company in the southern United States. Fearn's company repaired the river boat and sold it to W.C. Munn.

Fearn, his master shipwright, Thomas Palfrey, and veteran captains of Placentia, Captain George O'Reilly and Thomas Kemp, were called to testify.

One of the key pieces of evidence was a personal letter from a husband to his wife. Engineer Peter Stewart of St. John's wrote his wife before *Beverley* left Harbour Grace, saying in his letter that he had doubts about the seaworthiness of the ship. He was most concerned that a thirteen-inch leak had not been properly repaired. His letter was analysed in the proceedings.

At the enquiry, a list of crew was presented, but was not given orally for reporters to record nor was the list presented publically. However, the enquiry examined the story of three firemen, Thomas Carrigan, John Noftall, and John Power, who jumped ship a day or so before *Beverley* sailed. They merely wished during the delay in sailing to go home to visit family in St. John's before the ship departed.

While walking along a road just outside St. John's, they were apprehended by the local police and brought back to *Beverley* at Harbour Grace. Detective Whelan, who interviewed the three, was called to testify and present the interview he had with Carrigan, Noftall, and Power. Whelan stated that the seamen had not claimed *Beverley* was unseaworthy, nor had made any comment of the condition of the ship.

Anxiety For Vessels

The S. S. Beverley, Captain Wilson, is now out 38 days from Hr. Grace, fish laden by Munn & Co., for the other side. The gravest fears are en-

Anxiety for the whereabouts of the missing steamer *Beverley* surfaces publically. The *Evening Advocate* of February 28, 1918, speculates on what happened to *Beverley*, as well as the schooner *W.C. McKay*, captained by W. O'Neill. The latter left Twillingate for Gibraltar and had been gone for 100 days.

Before the ship sailed on what was to be its final voyage on January 23, 1918, the three men were handed over to *Beverley*'s Captain Wilson and they were taken aboard the ship in preparation for its fateful and final voyage.

Whelan testified the three did not believe they had deserted ship, but merely wished to go home for a day or so while waiting the departure of the steamer.

When the enquiry ended in late January 1919, it concluded that *Beverley*, an old and discarded American river boat built to carry passengers on the Mississippi River, had inappropriately been put to work in Newfoundland as a transatlantic cargo ship. It simply was not suitable for the rigours of the treacherous North Atlantic and should not have received a certificate of seaworthiness after repairs at Placentia.

However, many a seaworthy, staunch ves-

CREW OF S.S. *BEVERLEY*, MISSING SINCE JANUARY 1918

James Barrett
  husband of Mary Barrett, 13 Holloway St., St. John's
Frank Barron
  son of Kate Barron, Placentia
James Barron
  husband of Julia Barron, 2 Bannerman St., St. John's
Thomas Carrigan
  son of Catherine Carrigan, Logy Bay, 5 children
Richard Collins
  son of Sarah F. Collins, 7 Mullock St., St. John's
John Dodd
  son of John Dodd, 14 Boncloddy Street, St. John's
James Dooley
  husband of Margaret Dooley, 13 Barron St., St. John's
Robert Green
  husband of Priscilla Green, 85 King's Rd., St. John's
Fred Hann
  5 Spencer Street, St. John's
James Hearn
  son of Jane Hearn, Caul's Lane, St. John's
Patrick Hearn
  husband of Annie, Caul's Lane, St. John's
William Kenney
  husband of Annie Kenney, Duckworth St., St. John's
Cebos Lewis
  husband of Emma, Battery Road, St. John's
John Noftall
  husband of Margaret Noftall, 22 Casey St., St. John's
Cornelius Pender
  son of Ann Pender, 39 Plank Road, St. John's
John Power, Outer Cove
Albert Ryan
  son of John Ryan, St. Joseph's, Salmonier
Peter Stewart
  husband of Helen Stewart, 106 Water St., St. John's
Patrick Walsh
  husband of Veronica Walsh, 36 Casey St., St. John's
Capt. Andrew Wilson
  husband of Mary Wilson, 51 Carter's Hill, St. John's
Andrew Wilson
  son of Mary Wilson, 51 Carter's Hill, St. John's
John Cunningham, residence uncertain
Eli Peddle, residence uncertain
Andrew Devereaux, residence uncertain

sel had disappeared at sea. Defence lawyer Howley, in his summation on January 24, pointed out that *Beverley* may have gone down for a number of reasons: it could have struck a floating mine, been torpedoed by a submarine, collided with a derelict, or capsized in a gale of wind.

The court of enquiry wound down and memories of the steamship faded, but in August 1933, fifteen years after it disappeared, the story of *Beverley* once again resurfaced. A building commonly known as "Beverley House," situated off Molloy's Lane near Bowering Park, caught fire and burned to the ground.

The structure, the passenger house purchased from the S.S. *Beverley* by John Duff — the proprietor of Queen's Theatre — had been taken apart in sections and reconstructed off Molloy's Lane. Beverley House had been used as a hostel and then as rental units. Abandoned and dilapidated, fire finally destroyed what was left of the ill-fated ship on August 3, 1933. It had been sold to a farmer named Brennan a few days before the fire.

The last vestiges of a ship that took twenty-four lives from St. John's and area met a fiery end as the newspaper of August 4, 1933, reports.

Chapter 40

Mercy Missions of the Harbour Tug

"Many a seaman owes his life to this little ship."

That was how the newspaper *Daily News* described the role of the St. John's harbour tug *D.P. Ingraham*. In the thirty-three years of yeoman work around Newfoundland's stormy shores, the tug played a part in nearly every aspect of sea activity: Bait Protection Service, Revenue Service, Supreme Court on Circuit, search, rescue, towing, diving, and wrecking operations. The *Ingraham*, as it was often called, braved all weather and frequented nearly every coast to rescue and to bring scores of shipwrecked sailors to safety.

D.P. Ingraham, built in 1864 at Philadelphia out of the best American white oak and fastened with copper throughout, was first employed as a gun boat during the American Civil War. It was later purchased by a towing company at Port Morien, Nova Scotia. In 1888, Captain Green of St. John's bought the tug for the Newfoundland Tug Company.

Its first work upon arrival in Newfoundland was to tow Bowring's vessel *Mary Cory* to port. During the first week of July 1888, the *Ingraham* was sent to the south coast to enforce the provisions of the Bait Act; legislation designed to prevent foreign ships from taking capelin and squid from Newfoundland. The tug captured two French bankers — *Amazon* and *Virginia* — off Cape St. Mary's. They were towed into Placentia and their captains and crews of approximately thirty were imprisoned there until court proceedings began.

VARIOUS WRECKS

Throughout its long career the workhorse went to the site of many marine disasters. In May 1894, *D.P. Ingraham* steamed to Red Head, near Grate's Cove, to investigate the loss of the steamer *Calitro* that had wrecked in the night of May 18. (For the full story on *Calitro*, see book *Between Sea and Sky.*)

In September 1900, a devastating hurricane swept northern Newfoundland. Captain Cross of the *Ingraham* brought the shipwrecked crews of several vessels to home ports in Bonavista and Conception Bay.

From February 15-19, 1901, local papers ran several long columns on the pieces of a wreck that *D.P. Ingraham* brought to St. John's. Captain Lewis Young had been sent to Trinity Bay to investigate the wreckage which eventually proved to be the S.S. *Lucerne*, lost with all crew near Baccalieu Island. In January 1909, *Ingraham* was sent to Fortune Bay to search for the missing Grand Bank schooner *Vesta*.

Schooner *Souris Bell* ran aground and broke up outside the Narrows in 1909. Several of the crew who had climbed on pans of ice were rescued by the *Ingraham* as they drifted out to sea. Likewise the schooner *Reciprocity*, owned by Captain Jacob Kean of Wesleyville, wrecked in Freshwater Bay in May 1916. Its crew left in a small open boat and were drifting to sea when the *Ingraham*, alerted to the potential disaster, came by and pulled them to safely.

SHIP ASHORE AT INDIAN ISLAND

Two longer items illustrate the *Ingraham*'s role in shipping and rescue missions. On May 13, 1910, while attempting to navigate around Indian Island, Notre Dame Bay, the steamer *Louise* under Captain Baxter Barbour struck a rock about 200 yards off the eastern end of the island. Previously Barbour had gone to Indian Island by way of Indian Island Run, but thinking the water was shallow, he tried the Stag Harbour Run believing it was a better route.

As the ship steamed at a full speed of ten knots, it struck a rock or ledge not indicated on the captain's coastal charts. All stores and everything moveable were taken off the steamer to lighten it, but attempts to refloat the steamer failed.

An early photo of Fogo with Brimstone Head in the background centre. In the 1980s, the Flat Earth Society proclaimed Brimstone Head one of the four corners of the world.

By the next day, a westerly wind stirred up heavy seas and this pounded the ship on the rocks. The bottom was torn out and it seemed to the crew the vessel would break up. Barbour and his six men who had stayed with their ship had great difficulty abandoning the *Louise* as they had only a small boat for the heavy breakers. They donned lifebelts, eventually reached shore, and walked three miles to the settlement of Indian Island.

Wreck Commissioner A. Stone was given orders to sell the hulk. *D.P. Ingraham*, sent to bring the crew home, arrived back in St. John's from the Fogo area on May 18.

WRECK OF S.S. *LABRADOR*

In early March 1913, the James Baird business of St. John's learned their sealing ship S.S. *Labrador*, captained by D. Martin, had gone ashore at Branch, St. Mary's Bay, and the crew was safe. Immediately Baird notified Archibald Piccott, the Minister of Marine and Fisheries, who sent the tug *D.P. Ingraham* to see if the wreck could be pulled off and to bring *Labrador*'s crew home.

Built in 1866, the Bairds purchased the 256-ton S.S. *Labrador* in 1891. In 1892, under the command of Captain George Hann, it was the first to arrive in St. John's from the seal fishery loaded with pelts. In March 1896, still under Captain Hann, the ship brought home the crew of *Windsor Lake*, a sealing vessel lost about sixty miles from Cape Freels.

On Saturday, March 1, 1913, *Labrador* left St. John's for Codroy where it would clear for the seal fishery. En route the steamer was to stop at Trepassey where twenty men would sign on. By Sunday, the lighthouse keeper at Cape Race reported stormy weather and dense fog such that *Labrador* could not harbour in Trepassey. The steamer attempted to reach St. Lawrence, but on the way it grounded near Branch.

THE END OF A TUG

Ingraham's thirty-three-year career came to a disastrous end in December 1921. On December 5, *D.P. Ingraham* towed a coal laden tern schooner, the Grand Bank-owned *Jean & Mary*, down the Straight Shore on Newfoundland's Northeast coast. The tern was to deliver coal to Twillingate.

The crew of the St. John's harbour tug *D.P. Ingraham* (above) pose for a photo. Its first skipper was Captain C. Cross, followed by Lewis Young; then Captain Marmaduke "Duke" Rose commanded it for thirteen years to about 1918.

When wrecked on the Penguin Islands in 1921, *Ingraham*'s crew — Captain Charles Moore, mate George Fowlow, engineers W. Squires and George Hansford, fireman Henry Whitten, seamen Thomas Evans, John Piercey, and John Walsh — was rescued by the Penguin Island light keeper.

During a violent storm that night, the tug was wrecked on the North Penguin Island; *Jean & Mary* went to pieces on South Penguin Island and all crew perished: Captain Abe Tom Cluett of Belleoram; James Francis, Henry Lee and John Gould, Grand Bank; Charlie Follett and William Tapper of Grand Beach.

D.P. Ingraham standing by the wrecked *Elizabeth Fearn* after it went ashore at Quidi Vidi on February 12, 1921. Captain Vatcher and his eight crewmen rowed ashore safely. Photo courtesy of Michael Harrington.

Chapter 41

Tragedy at Bay Bulls

Bay Bulls/Conception Bay

Brigantine *Lavinia* discharged its cargo of fish at Leghorn, Italy, in early November 1865, and left on November 9 to sail to Cadiz, Spain. There the 126-ton ship took on salt to complete its cargo of marble and a few casks of wine destined for St. John's. In addition to Captain Mercer, mate Thomas Carrol, and the other six hands, *Lavinia* also had Mercer's wife — born in Shaldon, Devonshire, England — and their three year old child aboard.

Westward voyages in November were usually stormy; the Atlantic showed no mercy that time of year. Mercer and crew laboured all the way, fighting heavy gales, snow, and sleet. On December 21, the storm trysail burst in the force of wind, causing *Lavinia* to ship several successive large waves. The cargo shifted slightly, enough to put the brigantine on an uneven keel.

On the first day of the new year, 1866, conditions were no better; in fact they became progressively worse. A sea came on board, smashing the longboat to pieces and carrying away part of the bulwarks. By Thursday, January 11, Mercer figured he was nearing Newfoundland.

At 1 p.m. with a wind blowing strong from the southwest in driving sleet, the sails had to be double reefed. The ocean was covered with slob ice. The land sighted by the lookout was Bay Bulls North Head. Captain Mercer consulted his charts and chronometer and figured he should not have made this point for another six hours.

Was there time to heave the ship around to avoid trouble? The slob ice and slight list saw to that for *Lavinia* would not "stay." It struck rocks about a quarter of a mile to the south of North Head of Bay Bulls.

Lavinia's longboat was smashed and the crew prepared the jolly boat. The six crew, including the captain and mate, as well as Mrs. Mercer and child, climbed aboard. As soon as they pushed off from the vessel, they realized that eight people aboard the small craft was too much. In the slob ice and breakers, the jolly boat could not be manoeuvred properly through the ice.

While trying to keep the little craft off the land and ice-covered rocks, a wave struck the boat, breaking it in two pieces. All aboard were thrown into the water. Six succeeded in holding on the rocks and scrambled ashore, but mate Carrol, Captain Mercer, his wife and child disappeared from sight. Those watching from the rocks were helpless to assist. Carrol was seen struggling and was probably killed when the boat broke up on the ledge, but the other three disappeared. The survivors called and shouted but received no answer.

The shouting attracted the attention of John Hall, an Englishman who lived near North Head, Bay Bulls. He took the men to his home and gave them food and dry clothing. Otherwise they would have perished from exposure before they reached Bay Bulls.

By daybreak January 12, 1866, *Lavinia* had entirely gone to pieces and not a section of it remained; this despite the fact the ship was strong, well-built, and newly fitted with iron knees and stanchions.

Although the late Captain Mercer was young, he had the entire confidence of *Lavinia's* owners, J. & W. Stewart, and was highly regarded by many Newfoundland seamen. The shipping firm of J. & W. Stewart was founded by James Stewart who was born in Greenock, Scotland, and moved to Newfoundland. He was credited with being the first to trade fish with Brazil. His business lasted until the 1890s.

Several years later, J. & W. Stewart's shipping business was hit another devastating loss at sea. In a mid-September gale of 1891, the schooner *Percie*, commanded by John Cull Kane, was lost with crew. The crew of six or seven, nearly all related, belonged to Pound Cove, Trinity Bay, about nine miles from Greenspond.

Kane and his men had done well in the Labrador fishery and after landing the summer's catch had gone to the grounds off the Funk Islands. While returning from the Funks, *Percie* was overtaken by the sudden storm. In the same storm the schooner *Amazon*, captained by James Noble out of Fair Island, Bonavista Bay, was lost with three crew — Captain Noble and two men — Cutler and Wicks. *Royal Blue* went down as well, but all the crew was saved.

On November 17, 1950, the Halifax-based National Seafoods steam trawler *Flatholm* grounded and wrecked ten miles south of St. John's at Shoal Bay; a dent in the coastline between Petty Harbour and Bay Bulls. First to search for the trawler was Captain Arch Thornhill in the dragger *Blue Foam*, but in dense fog he could not locate the vessel. On November 19, it was learned Captain R. A. Winn and his nineteen crew rowed in safely to Bay Bulls. *Flatholm* was never refloated. Photo courtesy of Bruce Neal.

Chapter 42

Wrecks Along the Motion

Petty Harbour Motion/The Southern Shore

Petty Harbour, located at the head of Motion Bay, has North Head on one side and Motion Head on the other. In the era of sail, the more sheltered southern side was often referred to as Petty Harbour Motion. During the same time it was noted for the many wrecks that happened there.

In 1860, there were two ships lost in that area: *Caroline Schenck*, commanded by Captain Bond, was lost with all hands on October 3 while coming from Brazil to Newfoundland. Not long after P. & L. Tessier's ship *Kate Pendergast* was wrecked at Petty Harbour Motion while sailing from Demerara with a cargo of rum.

Within a week after this loss, another vessel hit the rocks at Stafford's Side, Petty Harbour. It was the brigantine *Spangle* en route from Sydney with coal. Captain James Lynch was in command and no lives were lost.

The strange fate of the schooner *Lizette* was a tale long remembered by the early settlers of Petty Harbour. On February 6, 1882, *Lizette* was caught in drift ice and was pushed in toward land between Bay Bulls and Petty Harbour. Some fishermen went out to help, but Captain Buttner refused to let them on board. Slowly the vessel drifted in, eventually striking Dick French's Rock, just inside Motion Head.

Watchers on the shore saw seas sweep over *Lizette* now separated from the land by a stretch of boiling seas, so mad and treacherous that the Petty Harbour men who came to the scene would not put out a small boat to cross it. One man, Jacob Chafe, brought his sealing gun and tried to fire a ramrod with a line attached across the gap. Each rod fell short, but he kept trying until he had used up all available rods in the town.

All this time *Lizette* was taking a beating from the seas and rocks. One comber which swept across the deck carried three men overboard, never to be seen again. Eventually a Petty Harbour fisherman located a cod jigger with a long jigger line attached to it. He stood out in the surf as far as he could and hurled the line towards the men. One seaman caught it and pulled in the line which by now had a heavier line attached.

Lizette's mate tied the line around his waist and the two remaining men clung to the mate. In this way all three were pulled to safety. The bodies of Buttner and the other crew of *Lizette* were never found.

RENEWS ROCK DISASTER

Another disastrous wreck occurred on the Southern Shore on June 9, 1873, when the *Memento*, captained by Fred Adams, struck Renews Rock and all crew perished. Captain Auchinleck, the captain's brother-in-law, sailed as mate on this voyage; others were Adams' son and four other seamen. According to oral family history, the son, age fifteen, was on his first sea voyage; his father was thirty-five.

Originally registered to Brooking and Company, at the time of the wreck *Memento* was owned by Edwin Duder. The schooner left St. John's on June 9 and within twenty-four hours it was a total loss.

Not much has been recorded of the circumstances of this disaster except for one piece of information. On August 16, 1873, an article appeared in *The Patroit and Catholic Herald*, detailing the finding of one of the bodies from *Memento*:

> On Monday, August 11, an inquest was held before Dr. Renouf, Coroner, at the house of Mr. Maurice Goff in Casey's Lane on view of the body of Patrick Lawlor, age forty-nine years, a fish culler and passenger on board the schooner *Memento*, belonging to Edwin Duder esq., which vessel left here on the 9th of June last, bound to Rose Blanche for a cargo of fish.
>
> It is supposed the vessel must have struck on Renews Rock that night and sank in deep water with all hands on board — seven in number. The body was observed floating in the vicinity of the rock by some fishermen on Friday last, and immediately conveyed it here. It was very much decomposed, particularly the face and hands. The clothes and contents of pockets were recognized by his brother and his wife as belonging to her late husband. The jury returned a verdict of "Found Drowned." He leaves a wife and five young children.

Duder's business once had more than 200 vessels on Lloyd's register, the largest fleet ever registered in Newfoundland and is said to be the largest in the world at that time. In 1871, Edwin Duder, Jr. joined his father's firm and on his father's death in 1881, took control of the business, expanding it to Twillingate, Fogo, Herring Neck, and Change Islands.

Duder's success did not last long. By 1894, he was deeply in debt to the Commercial Bank and, following the Bank Crash of 1894, his company went bankrupt. Duder faded from the business world and his waterfront premises were eventually taken over by others.

ONE OF THE WORST CASES OF SUFFERING

When the story of the wreck of the barquentine *Vidonia* was told around the homes of Petty Harbour, people said that it was one of the worst cases of human suffering and hardship ever endured by Newfoundland seamen.

Vidonia, a wooden barquentine of 206 gross tons, was 114 feet long and was built in 1877. It had sailed for Brazil with a cargo of cod in drums and half drums.

On February 10, 1905, disaster overtook Captain Job Vine and Captain William Martin when *Vidonia* hit French's Rock and the line of sunkers between Long Point and Motion Head. During a vicious blinding storm when the bay was filled with loose slob ice, the ship had been forced in near shore by contrary winds and closely packed with slob ice.

The eight crew stayed on board for an hour, but were forced to abandon ship when *Vidonia* began to break apart. They had to place boards before them and crawl on their hands and knees over the soft ice as a howling wind-storm and bitter temperatures accosted them.

Finally, wet and cold, they breached the quarter of a mile gap to the rocks, but there was not a house nor building in sight. For two nights and a day without a scrap of food, they crouched near a boulder and suffered. At daylight the second day, two men became delirious and finally unconscious with exhaustion. No doubt the situation would have been worse except that seaman Sweeney from Carbonear, sang, joked and forced the others to endure and stay awake. Sweeney made them dance and walk to keep the circulation up and cheered them on.

With a break in the wind and snow, they left to walk to Petty Harbour at 6 a.m. By this time there was no sign of *Vidonia* and the crew figured it had split in two and sunk. Not knowing which way to walk, they often lost their way and had to retrace their steps. By this time the ship's bosun was near death. Captain Vine's hands were so sore and swollen from frost, he could not keep his mitts on.

Finally eight hours later they were met by Mr. J.W. Chafe and a man named Weir. These men had dogs and sleighs with them and carried the shipwrecked men to Petty Harbour. Captain Vine phoned the news to the Bowerings. The families of Hannaford, Chafe and Lee gave them lodging while Weir went to St. John's with a letter to Mrs. Vine, informing her the men were suffering but alive.

Captain Martin later commanded the Red Cross liner *Florizel* and was captain when it was wrecked at Cappahayden on February 24, 1918. Ninety-four lost their lives; Captain Martin survived.

THE SCENE OF THE WRECK

On July 17, 1922, the Lunenburg schooner *Doris L. Corkum* was stranded three miles east of Cape Ballard at Small Point. The crew, nearly all Nova Scotians, left the wreck without mishap; however, the ninety-eight-ton schooner had a fine catch of fish stored in the holds.

When it became known around the coast a banker was ashore, scores of local motor boats — many from Renews, Fermeuse and vicinity — went to the scene to salvage what fish they could. Nearly 100 boats were at the wreck site including the small banker *Viator*, owned and captained by Eliol Hiscock of Winterton, Trinity Bay, who fished out of Fermeuse.

Captain Hiscock and his eighteen year old son Peter figured a dory would be easier to handle near the wreck site. They put one over the side and approached the abandoned *Doris L. Corkum*. At that particular moment when *Viator*'s dory was near the hull, a sea struck the stranded schooner, throwing the ship over on its side. As it fell, the main boom swung over the ship's side, struck Captain

Hiscock in the head and killed him instantly. His body fell into the water near the dory.

Peter Hiscock helped recover his father's body. It was taken by the tug *Hugh D* to St. John's where undertaker Murphy arranged to send the remains to Trinity Bay. The captain was fifty-eight and married with seven children.

Chapter 43

Anxious Times for Letty B

Cape Broyle/Trepassey

When the train from Trepassey pulled into St. John's on January 26, 1928, one of the passengers was Austin Carew, captain of the Cape Broyle schooner *Letty B*. For several days the people of Cape Broyle had not heard from Austin nor his schooner. *Letty B* had been first registered to Ernest Carew, but when he passed away in 1916, ownership went to his wife, Sarah Carew.

Situated on the east coast about halfway between St. John's and Cape Race, Cape Broyle has several distinctions: it is one of the oldest towns in Newfoundland with the first recorded settlement in 1618. Census returns for 1696 show thirteen residents and in the 1700s there was an influx of Irish fishermen/farmers. Always dependant upon the sea, the town diversified from cod in 1903 and opened a whaling factory. In the era of sail, Cape Broyle workers sold bait and ice to American, Canadian, and Newfoundland banking schooners. Today the town has a population of about 700.

Letty B left St. John's on Tuesday evening, January 17, for the run south to Cape Broyle; a destination easily reached in an afternoon with favourable winds. Aboard were Austin Carew, age twenty-three; James Carew, twenty; and Stephen Yard, twenty-two — a youthful crew, but one which could handle adverse conditions as they were soon to find out. James and Austin's father, James, had died and both boys were helping support a family of eleven.

About 8:30 p.m., when the schooner was off Petty Harbour Motion, the wind, with a little snow, came up from the northeast forcing the crew to run up nearly parallel to the shore. They kept the little schooner about three and a half miles off. When the wind veered south southeast, snowfall increased to a blizzard.

At 11 p.m. the jib was carried away, the bowsprit broke, and the main sail went in two pieces. By Wednesday morning, *Letty B* lay to off Cape Ballard with the wind from the south. All that day and Thursday, Carew and the other two seamen looked for land.

During a lull in a snow squall, they saw what appeared to be Cape Race, but there was nothing to be done in the wind but wait. On Friday Carew ran in for land, but again in the gale had to lie to under a double-reefed foresail.

During these three days, the people of Cape Broyle, knowing *Letty B* had left for home, frantically wired St. John's and Cape Race for news on the schooner. No one there knew much about the schooner except that it left port on Tuesday. Every day practically everyone in the community gathered at the Carew home to pray. The priest also visited twice a day while the schooner was missing.

Now at daylight on Saturday, January 21, and off Cape Race, the two Carews and Yard tried the pumps and although they seemed to be working fine, they could hear water sloshing around in the holds. Two hours worth of pumping couldn't keep down the inflow; *Letty B* was slowly sinking.

They prepared the dory and went below one last time to check the water level; it was now up over the top bunks. At 8 a.m. they boarded the dory and abandoned *Letty B*. The young men shaped a course northwest by north and, after rowing from 8 to 1 p.m., finally sighted Cape Pine.

Three exhausted shipwrecked seamen rowed into Trepassey at 8 p.m., after twelve hours of rowing in heavy wind. The dory was half full of water. Despite a long pull in cold weather, the only damage was to Austin Carew's feet, both frostbitten. The Trepassey telegraph office wired news of their safe arrival to St. John's where it was relayed to Cape Broyle. *Letty B*'s crew left on the next train from Trepassey to St. John's.

There to meet them at the train station was Major Peter J. Cashin and Philip F. Moore, the two governmental representatives for Ferryland district which includes Cape Broyle. They accompanied Captain Carew to the General Hospital for treatment for his feet.

Cape Broyle also has the distinction of being the birthplace of Sir Michael P. Cashin who became Prime Minister of Newfoundland in 1919. It was his son, Major Peter who met the shipwrecked crew at St. John's.

Austin Carew sailed on the Nova Scotian schooner *Bluenose* for awhile, but in later life developed severe arthritis as a result of his hardships on the sea. Stephen Yard lost his life during World War II on a merchant marine ship.

WRECK OF THE *MARY M. BELTEN*

Two years later in 1930, during a fierce November storm, the schooner *Mary M. Belten* ran into difficulty off Church Cove, Cape Broyle. The master and owner of the schooner was William Croft of Aquaforte. With him were his two sons, James, age twenty-five, Bernard, twenty-two, and his brother George.

While Croft was lowering the foresail of the schooner with the intention of using the engine, a high wave hit *Mary M. Belten*. The vessel fell on its side, the cargo shifted, and kept it keeled over. The four crew were washed overboard with the same sea. Bernard Croft managed to grab the main boom and caught the dory which was nearby.

Bernard tied the painter to the rigging and while he was in the act of getting his father out of the water and into the dory, a second sea swept the dory away with the two men in it. They could see James Croft clinging to the cross trees of the schooner, but couldn't rescue him. There was only one oar left in the dory and with the high winds the two survivors couldn't get back to rescue James.

George Croft was caught under the foresail in the water and could not free himself. Father and son drifted on the rocks and barely escaped with their lives. They had to journey three miles in wet clothing through woods during a wild storm before they reached some houses on the Calvert side. William Croft and his son Bernard gave the alarm their schooner was ashore in Church Cove, but were too weak from exposure to go to the site. Ferryland's Police Sergeant O'Flaherty notified authorities in St. John's.

In the wreck, the Crofts lost all winter supplies, but more tragic, two lives: George Croft of Aquaforte who left a wife and eleven children, the eldest about seventeen years old. James Croft was single.

Rupert Brand III (above) aground and a total loss near St. Shotts February 23, 1964. Photo courtesy of Dave Piercey, Fortune.

Rupert Brand III, a 115-ton dragger, was registered in Vancouver and operated at the time of its loss by B.C. Packers fish plant in Harbour Breton. Photo courtesy of Dave Piercey, Fortune.

Two lifeboats of the wrecked *Rupert Brand III*. Captain Thomas Kearley, engineer Roland Matthews and crew all escaped safely. They went to St. Shotts where the people took in the stranded seamen. Photo courtesy of Dave Piercey, Fortune.

Chapter 44

A Survivor's View of Newfoundland, 1917

Cape Race/St. John's

The capital city of Norway was once called Kristiania (after King Kristian), but in 1925 the name officially changed to Oslo. When a new passenger liner slipped down the ways at Birkenhead, England, in 1913, it had been named *Kristianiafjord* after the city, Kristiania, with the word fjord being equivalent to a long narrow bay in which the city is located.

Built for Norwegian American Liners, the ship was 530 feet long, compared to *Titanic*'s nearly 900 feet. By 1917, *Kristianiafjord* had made many transatlantic voyages and was considered the flag or "star" liner in the fleet.

It left New York on July 7, 1917, and stopped at Halifax, one of its regular ports of call. When the steamer departed for the eastward voyage across the Atlantic on July 13, it carried 900 passengers and 250 crew, plus a substantial load of freight destined for Belgium.

Three passengers were the Norenius children: Nils, age fourteen, Sigrid, thirteen, and Karin, eleven. Karin kept a diary or record of their journey from South Africa to Sweden and described the unscheduled stopover in Newfoundland. Karin writes:

> My father and mother were Swedish missionaries to the Zulu people of South Africa and as mission chil-

dren, my brother and sister and I were sent back to
Sweden for schooling. We left Durban, South Africa,
May 3, 1917, on the Swedish steamer *Baltic* and
made several stops along the route; at South America,
Cuba, and New Orleans. At New Orleans, we trav-
elled by train to New York and boarded the liner
Kristianiafjord...

We hugged the coast up to Halifax, steaming into
the harbour to pick up passengers. When we left
Halifax a few days later, all the rats jumped overboard
— a bad sign, according to the sailors. Sigrid and I
shared a cabin with two missionary ladies. During the
day, we could go on deck but at nightfall everyone
had to be inside with no lights on deck at all.

Above *Kristianiafjord* is bedecked with flags on its 1913 launch day with the flag of Norway
on the stern.
    Although there was no loss of life when the great liner went ashore, on August 8, 1917,
Patrick D. Curtis died while working at the site. He and Silas Perry were climbing a steel wire
hanging over the hull of the wreck when the line let go. Curtis fell into the sea and drowned.
Photo courtesy of Hubert Hall, SHIPSEARCH Marine.

The great liner was travelling with "lights out" at night;
a safeguard against enemy submarines patrolling the
Atlantic. But it was not a hostile sub that caused the
demise of *Kristianiafjord*. In the foggy night of July 14,

1917, a strong inset of tide did its dirty work as *Kristianiafjord* passed near Cape Race. At 4 a.m. the steamer struck the rocks off Bob's Cove, located about seven miles west of Cape Race. The wireless station at Cape Race received the distress signal as did other vessels in the area, including S.S. *Stanley* and the Newfoundland ship *Sable Island.*

Before the two rescue ships arrived on the scene, all passengers were put aboard lifeboats and were taken into Bob's Cove, which at that time was inhabited by a few fishermen and their families. When the S.S. *Sable Island*, en route to St. John's came by, it took *Kristianiafjord's* women and children to St. John's. The first news release from St. John's on the wreck read:

> Norwegian steamer *Kristianiafjord* ashore seven miles west of Cape Race. Master reports landing passengers and requesting assistance. Canadian steamer *Stanley* standing by and sending steamers *Portia* and *Petrel.*

No doubt the American, Canadian, and European passengers landed on shore got a good look at Bob's Cove, Newfoundland, on that July 15 day. It's a small inlet in a rugged coast, exposed to all wind and sea, and has a shore line nearly void of vegetation except for bog and marshland stretching for miles. There is no record if the visitors climbed the seventy-foot cliff of shale and boulders to the top to view the shrub and stunted trees. Karin Norenius wrote:

> We were awaken by a terrific BANG, with sirens screaming and pandemonium all round — our boat had run aground into rocks. The two ladies in our room left and I had to battle to get Sigrid out of bed. We dressed quickly. We had had the lifeboat drill so we knew where to go and got into our lifeboat just as they were lowering it.

Many women had not dressed properly and were clad in just nighties; some had babies and children with them. There was a small fishing village nearby where we all landed. It was cold and miserable and all of us were suffering with shock. My sister and I were glad to see our brother safely on land.

We spent a cold miserable day on land, but late afternoon a small steamer passed and was commandeered to take as many women and children as possible to St. John's.

The ship Karin refers to was the S.S. *Sable Island*. When the tug *Petrel* arrived on the scene on July 17, it made a feeble attempt to tow *Kristianiafjord* off the rocks; but authorities soon requested larger salvage tugs. When tugs arrived from Halifax, divers surveyed the bottom and reported, "The vessel is resting on an even bottom and not straining much. Some damage was found under Number 2 and 4 holds, but the engine room, stokehold, and rest of hull apparently undamaged."

By July 20-21 much cargo had been removed. Divers had closed the holes. The work of salving cargo fell to small Newfoundland schooners and steamers. Stevedore T. Godden of St. John's had twenty experienced men and supervised the transfer of the cargo to steamers *Trembly* and *Ranger*. In time even the copper and lead cargo was taken off, but the powerful Halifax tugs needed more than time. Even with two weeks and calm seas at their disposal, it was futile — *Kristianiafjord* would never be refloated.

The great Norwegian American liner, now declared a total loss, was sold by public auction. The Honourable Michael Patrick Cashin bought the hulk for $2600. Before the wreck was finally claimed by the sea, one man lost his life. On August 7, Patrick Curtis of Trepassey drowned near the wreck of *Kristianiafjord*.

Many well-to-do people travelled on *Kristianiafjord* since the ship, considered a "neutral flag" vessel, was relatively safe from enemy attack. Norway was a neutral country in World War I and its ships were not targets for enemy U-boats. But in the end, of course, it was not an enemy torpedo that finished the liner, but the coastal rocks of Newfoundland.

When the stranded passengers arrived in St. John's, various charitable service organizations swung into action. Many women and children were lodged in the Seaman's Institute on Water Street. First class passengers stayed at the Princess Rink, once located behind present-day Fairmont Hotel or in the Grenfell Hall, and British Hall.

However, Karin Norenius recalled staying elsewhere:

> We arrived in the morning and were herded into a huge building where the residents of St. John's offered their help to us all. Two ladies heard that there were three Norenius children in the group. Something clicked in their minds that they had met a pastor Norenius in England who was studying English before going to South Africa as a missionary years ago. Could these be his children? And we were.
>
> The ladies took Sigrid and me to their home and Nils stayed with the Mayor and his family. The two ladies were very good to us which helped us get over the shock.

Unfortunately Karin did not record the names of the family who gave them lodging in St. John's. Her brother stayed in the home of St. John's Mayor William Gilbert Gosling (whose term of mayorship was 1914-1921).

Personal items belonging to the passengers taken from the wreck were brought to St. John's by the steamer *Prospero* and tug *Petrel*. Two thousand suitcases and trunks were landed at Shea's and Crosbie's waterfront premises where *Kristianiafjord*'s passengers (many of whom could speak no English) lined up to claim their belongings.

On August 5, the Swedish American vessel *Stockholm*, which had been in Halifax, steamed into St. John's to carry the shipwrecked people to Halifax and from there to Gothenburg, Sweden. Before leaving, they thanked the Government of Newfoundland, the people of St. John's as well as the residents of the southern shore for the kind treatment given them in Newfoundland. Karin writes:

> During the week in St. John's, most of the passengers' luggage was rescued. After a week there a passenger steamer came to pick us all up and took us back to Halifax. The beautiful Swedish steamer *Drottingholm* was there ready for us to embark and the crew of the wrecked *Kristianiafjord* were happy to get back to Sweden earlier than they thought. The passengers were also grateful to get aboard and settled down for a safe trip home.
>
> We passed along Newfoundland safely this time and went up further north then turning towards the Norwegian coast down to Gothenburg. There we were met by endless small and big boats with all kinds of flags flying and hooters going and people waving.

Chapter 45

For the Want of a Lighthouse

Many years ago a shipwreck at Trepassey spurred concerned citizens to renew their argument for an adequate beacon light to be placed on Powel's Point (today known as Powles or Powel's Head). The people of Trepassey claimed a lighthouse was sorely needed as a guide for vessels trying to enter the harbour. Trepassey, one of the first harbours of an easy access to vessels rounding Cape Race, was ice free and a relatively safe refuge.

In a letter to *The Evening Telegram* in October 1883, concerned citizens outlined these points and said that in the winter a large number of ships used Trepassey's safe confines and that sea traffic had been increasing in volume for several years. The whistle buoy, they said, placed near the harbour was "a poor makeshift for a lighthouse" and did little to help vessels.

On October 30, 1883, a ship sailed for Powel's Point with the intention of keeping west and entering Trepassey; however in the darkness and the storm, it sailed east of the point right into a small inlet called Sheep's Cove, near Trepassey. This cove is so named as years ago sheep let out in the spring to pasture on the point would wander into the cove looking for new growth of kelp on the rocks.

The entrance by sea to Trepassey harbour is formed by Powel's Point or Head and the western coastline of

Cape Pine. The entrance is narrow, about three quarters of a mile in width. In the days when there was no lighthouse, finding the entrance in thick fog or a blizzard would be a near impossible task.

The ship which again raised the plea for a decent light on the head was the bark *Jane Hunter*, owned by Walter Grieve and Company of St. John's. His ship cleared the Custom's House in St. John's on August 10, with the first cargo of new fish for Brazil. On the return voyage from Pernambuco, just as the long voyage ended and the shores of Newfoundland came in sight, *Jane Hunter* came to grief.

Aboard was one of the most knowledgeable and experienced ship masters in his day — Captain Henry Bowden of St. John's. For many years he commanded J. & W. Stewart's brig *Glaucus*. With Bowden were his mate Moses Roberts, William Seymour, Angus McDonald, Angus Wallace, William Tobin, David Taylor, Angus Rowe, and Alexander Downey.

For six days in October, as they approached Newfoundland, the captain could not take off his course by sextant. A storm shut out the sun by day and the stars at night; Bowden sailed by dead reckoning and didn't realize he was so near land. Downey, on look out duty, heard the captain comment that they were not less than twenty or thirty miles east of Cape Race.

The ship *Jane Hunter* was probably put on a northeast by east course to bring it into Trepassey. About 6 p.m. Downey saw a light and called the captain. The crew, believing they were well out from land, figured it to be a steamer's light. Bowden altered the course one point more easterly to east northeast.

It was on this course and less than an hour later when *Jane Hunter* hit land. One of the sailors said after, "The light must have been the Cape Pine light and we passed close to it in the pitch blackness of dense fog, rain in torrents, and a southeasterly gale."

By the time the crew figured it was the Cape Pine light, they were on the inside of it, not outside, and running dead toward land at about seven or eight knots an hour. Alexander Downey recalled:

> When the vessel struck, it was with such violence that the bottom must have been torn out. All hands were on deck. We had suspected no danger and the crash was a shock of terror to all. The sea was heaving in huge waves and this instantly engulfed the wreck.
>
> There was not a moment of time to get the ship's boat to rights, with the inky blackness of the night and the overwhelming heave of the surge.

Downey jumped for his life. He thought from his position on the bow he could see a faint sign of land. He was a good swimmer, but the rollers breaking on shore kept him under water nearly all the time. "When I rose to the surface," he said, "I only had time to fill my lungs with air and I was again swamped beneath the boiling breakers."

Each time Downey came close to the shore, the rebound of an immense wave carried him off again. But he fought desperately for his life until he gained a footing on the bottom and staggered ashore numb and exhausted. He saw none of his eight shipmates in the water while he was struggling to get ashore.

The distance between the spot where Downey leaped into the water and the shore was about fifty yards, but it took him a quarter of an hour before he made it across this short breach of mad ocean. He was safe on land but the weather — wind, fog, rain — was terrible and decreased his odds of survival. Downey recalled:

> I found shelter from the downpour of rain under some bushes while the stormy sea pounded on the beach. At last I heard a voice calling aloud through the darkness, 'Is anyone saved?' and I answered back. This was Angus Rowe. He had been washed ashore a quarter of a mile from where I was.

The two survivors waited and searched on the shore-line for shipmates, but there was no one else. The storm clouds moved aside and one by one the stars came out. By this dim light Downey and Rowe could barely recognize, from the appearance of the land, that they were near a set-tlement. They followed a trail leading across a neck of land, about a quarter of a mile in width which divides Trepassey harbour from Sheep's Cove, and reached the first house about 9 a.m.

Immediately the two survivors were taken into Trepassey homes and cared for. A search party left to locate the wreck of *Jane Hunter* and to find any other survivors or bodies.

While there is probably no photo of *Jane Hunter* circa 1883, this is a grounding of more recent vintage. Auxiliary schooner *Maggie Walsh* (above) is stranded at North West Cove, Trepassey, in 1956. It delivered cargo from St. John's to Newfoundland's southern shore. The thirty-three-feet long *Maggie Walsh*, built at Fermeuse in 1940, was owned by Nicholas Walsh. Photo courtesy of Bruce Neal.

Within a day four bodies from *Jane Hunter* were found; the next day one more was located. Captain Dowden's and the mate's remains were coffined and transported to St. John's. The final words of the tragedy which claimed seven lives come from the late Captain Bowden's interment announcement:

> On November 6, 1883, the remains of the late Captain Bowden, who was a long-standing member of the Masonic Order (St. John's Lodge), of the ill-starred *Jane Hunter* were interred in the Church of England cemetery, St. John's. The funeral procession left the Masonic Hall, British Square; it consisted of relatives, friends, and the Masonic fraternity. At the cemetery the Reverend A. Heygate, senior curate of the Cathedral conducted the burial service. The Brethren of the "Mystic Tie" returned to their lodge room. So mote it be.

And what of Trepassey's plea for a lighthouse? Nineteen years later, in 1902, after a number of shipwrecks and various complaints from shipowners and area residents, the Newfoundland government installed a light at Powel's Head. The wooden tower, replaced later by an iron structure, stood until 1960; then a modern facility housed both the light and a fog alarm.

Chapter 46

Mall Bay to the Rescue

Mall Bay/Fortune

Over the course of Newfoundland's marine history, scores of ships left their bones along the southern end of the Avalon Peninsula; part of the lure and legend of the "Irish Loop" details the tales of ships and wrecks. Main shipping routes to and from Newfoundland, Europe, and North America lie in close proximity to that coast.

Scattered around the headlands, especially in the corners and coves of Cape St. Mary's, Cape Freels, and Cape Race, are the remains of many of these ships, large and small. Rarely though did sailing vessels venture off course enough to send them fleeing into Shoal Bay, St. Mary's Harbour or Mall Bay to the westward of Cape Race.

However, in February 1927, the residents of Mall Bay, a town located in an inlet bearing the same name on the eastern side of St. Mary's Bay, were surprised to find seven men knocking on their doors and asking for help. And help they got.

The schooner *Evelyn V. Miller*, a well-constructed schooner of ninety-nine tons and designed for the coasting trade, was owned by E. Parsons of Sydney, Nova Scotia. On its final voyage it carried 450 casks of oil loaded at Halifax and slated to be landed at the Imperial Oil Company Yards in St. John's. Captain George Elford of Fortune commanded *Evelyn V. Miller* with a crew from his home town.

Off the southcoast of Newfoundland Elford sailed through a typical winter storm of thick snow pushed by a southeast gale. At 3 p.m. on Monday, February 21, *Evelyn V. Miller* passed Point La Haye in St. Mary's Bay. When the skipper attempted to tack off the point, the schooner struck a ledge and grounded at the base of a cliff north of Point La Haye, not far from Mall Bay.

The crew had a difficult time getting to the shore, but eventually climbed the snow and ice-covered cliff and walked five miles to the town of Mall Bay, reaching there in the night.

Mall Bay was first recorded separately in the 1845 *Census* with eighteen residents. Local tradition has it that an Irishman, one John Welsh from County Kerry, established a farm there in 1788. He was soon joined by another Irish farmer, Harry Fuher (Fewer) and what a character he was — stories of his exploits still exist today. Fewer once saved the life of a shipwrecked sailor and for some diabolical reason gave him a map, showing the location of a treasure buried in Mall Bay. The treasure was said to be guarded by a headless spirit. Over the years there have been many unsuccessful efforts to find the booty.

In the late 1800s, other families like Christophers and O'Rourkes settled there followed by Daleys, Meehans, Daltons, Nolans, and Dobbins — families who worked in the lobster, capelin, salmon, and cod fishery. By the 1920s the population held at over 100; today, with the downturn in the economy, Mall Bay has about sixty people.

Indeed the hardy fisher families of Mall Bay answered the call when shipwrecked strangers from *Evelyn V. Miller* came knocking on their doors. In the March 9 edition of the *Daily News* a commentary on the wreck said, "The people of Mall Bay treated the shipwrecked crew with every kindness, doing all possible to make them comfortable."

By Tuesday evening, February 22, the weather moderated and the work of salvaging began. The crew, assisted by those living in the area and James Tobin, the local customs and salvage supervisor, recovered and stacked on shore one spar, all the booms, gaffs and canvas. As well, most of the drums of oil were recovered. On Thursday, four days after *Evelyn V. Miller* grounded, the schooner was smashed to matchwood by heavy seas; the anchors and chains remained on the bottom near the wreck site.

Seeing nothing further could be done, Elford and his crew went to St. Mary's where they joined the coastal steamer *Portia*. At Argentia they took the train to St. John's, arriving on Monday, February 28, seven days after the wreck of *Evelyn V. Miller* at Mall Bay.

Chapter 47

A St. Mary's Hero

In the era of sail-driven fishing schooners, American and Nova Scotian salt fish companies sent their ships to the prolific grounds off the southern Avalon. Schooner captains were inclined to hire the local men of the south coast who not only knew the area, but were experienced and hardy fishermen.

Often, it was only when a ship was lost that the roster of Newfoundland fishermen was published. For example, in April 1895, when the Gloucester banking schooner *Mildred W. Lee* wrecked near the Bay of Fundy, its entire sixteen crew drowned. Eight of those, all single, were from Newfoundland: George Grant of Burgeo; brothers Thomas and Richard Williams, Fenwick Williams, Bay Bulls; Michael Connolly, Tors Cove; Lawrence King, St. Mary's; John Carey, Witless Bay; and Patrick Fahey of Fermeuse. Fahey's parents and siblings lived in Blackstone, Massachusetts.

When the Lunenburg schooner *Joyce C. Smith*, disappeared with crew in the August gales of 1928, the banker carried seventeen Newfoundland crew including fourteen from the Burin area. One of the last wooden schooners out of Gloucester, the *Mary O'Hara*, grounded and was wrecked near Boston on January 21, 1941. Several of the men died of exposure, including Thomas Moulton of Lewin's Cove, and John Sheehan of Bay

Bulls, who were both living in the United States at the time.

In June 1915, the Gorton Pew Fish Company's schooner *Flirtation* was based in St. Mary's Bay. It is not known how many Newfoundland workers were on *Flirtation*, but there were at least four: Captain Charles Daly, mate Joseph Daly, of Riverhead/St. Mary's, dorymen Austin Breen and James Yetman, both of St. Mary's. Breen was the dory "skipper" with Yetman his dory mate.

On June 23, Breen's dory was out longer than expected. Captain Daly, uneasy about the delay, went with the mate up in the rigging to scan the horizon. They saw the dory in the distance about two points to the leeward and watched it for awhile.

The dory was slowly making its way toward the mother ship, but appeared to be too deeply laden for the sea that was running with large breaking swells and white caps. When the dory was about a quarter of a mile from *Flirtation*, a large wave upset the little craft, throwing both men into the water.

The schooner could not be swung around in time; thus there was nothing to be done except to launch a dory to get to them as soon as possible. Daly and the mate manned the rescue boat and unshipped the oars. As they were nearing the overturned dory, they could see young Yetman on the bottom of it, but they could not see Austin Breen.

He was on the other side, partly submerged, but barely alive and clinging onto the gunwale (or gunnel) which was under water. When the rescuers were within hailing distance, Breen shouted to the captain, "Save Jim! I'm all right!"

But these were his last words for he died of hypothermia before he could be rescued. Later Captain Daly spoke on the heroism of Austin Breen, saying,

> Fancy, a man saying he was all right, holding a dory's
> gunnel which was under water. Breen could have eas-

ily have gotten on the bottom of the dory, but he knew
by doing do, he would probably drown his weakened
dory mate and maybe himself too. A dory bottom-up
is poor comfort in a heavy sea. But Austin faced his
task like a man to save a human life.

Austin Breen of St. Mary's was twenty-six years old
and married. Yetman was twenty-two and single. So it was
in the era when American fishing schooners visited
Newfoundland villages. They provided employment, but
the treacherous sea and the hazards of bank fishing took
a terrible wage in lost lives.

Chapter 48

A Long Row to Safety

Golden Bay to North Harbour, St. Mary's Bay

Often in the tales of shipwreck and survival we think of vessels lost on foreign shores, of sailors struggling for survival in a strange land, fighting the elements in unfamiliar waters. But sometimes even Newfoundland's shores were equally inhospitable as this yarn of the sea shows.

On the evening of March 2, 1926, while attempting to navigate along the southern Avalon through dense fog, the schooner *Amy Stella*, one of the foreign-going fleet of ships operated by the Fishermen's Protective Union (FPU) in Port Union, sailed into a nest of rocks off Golden Bay near Cape St. Mary's. This vessel was built in Holland in 1918 and first carried the name

---

NOTICE.

I, G. C. Harris, of Marystown, Newfoundland; hereby give notice that in consequence of change of trade, I have applied to the Board of Trade, under Section 47 of the Merchant Shipping Act, 1894, in respect of the ship Lillian, of St. John's, Newfoundland, official number 134,926, of gross tonnage 129.83 tons, register tonnage 95.54 tons, heretofore owned by Josiah Hiscock of Grand Bank, Newfoundland; for permission to change her name to Ewart Harris, and to have her registered in the new name at the Port of St. John's, Newfoundland, as owned by Marystown Trading Company, Limited.

Any objections to the proposed change of name must be sent to the Registrar of Shipping at St. John's, Newfoundland, within seven days from the appearance of the advertisement.

Dated at St. John's, Newfoundland, this 25th day of September, 1916.

sep30,21

Notice of Name Change To change the name of a schooner, the owner had to give notice to the Board of Trade, Merchant Shipping Act, and it had to be publicized in a newspaper. On September 30, 1916, George C. Harris of Marystown/Grand Bank gave notice in the *Daily News* that his ninety-five-ton schooner *Lillian* of the Marystown Trading Company, had its name changed to *Ewart Harris*. The schooner had been previously owned by Josiah Hiscock of Grand Bank.

Elle. It was purchased by the FPU and eventually renamed *Amy Stella*.

The final voyage began in January. *Amy Stella* sailed to Brazil, discharged cargo, and loaded ballast for the trip north on February 2. Captain Wes Green commanded the vessel and he had a crew of Trinity Bay seamen with him.

While off Newfoundland, a winter storm battered the ship for several days. Before the vessel struck the shoals off Golden Bay, Captain Green ordered out the anchor, but he knew that unless the wind changed there was no way he could save his ship. About two in the morning the seven crew prepared the lifeboat as wind and seas pushed *Amy Stella* onto the rocks.

Once the lifeboat was over the side, the crew realized from the pounding surf they could not land at Golden Bay. Even with the wind in their favour, the haul around Point Lance taxed their energy. But before noon the next day, they were around the point and then tried to reach the town of Branch on the western side of St. Mary's Bay.

In an interview with the men after they reached home, the local paper said that:

> The seas were raging, in fact they were breaking over the high cliffs near Branch. All this time the lifeboat was continually shipping water and its occupants — those not rowing — kept themselves from being swamped by bailing out the boat with their hats and caps as seas broke over the lifeboat.

There was no way they could get into Branch so the crew put up a small sail, headed northeastward, and again attempted to reach land at Admiral's Beach, near Colinet Island. But "even this failure did not dampen the spirits of the hardy seamen, who were suffering untold hardships, as every man was wet from head to foot." They no choice only to continue sailing and rowing until they found a suitable place to land.

Finally on the west side of St. Mary's Bay, they ran up to the beach near Big Barachois River in a place called

Red Lane Cove. The shipwrecked men had tried to get to land in three places and succeeded on the fourth; Golden Bay, Branch, Admiral's Beach and the final stop at Big Barachois River on late Wednesday evening March 3.

At last, dry land — they had travelled by rowing and sailing over twenty-five miles "as the crow flies," but nearly twice that distance by sea. They managed this feat in an open boat in rough seas along an unfamiliar shore. When they stepped on land, even the act of getting out of the boat was fraught with danger:

> There were breakers ahead near shore, but *Amy Stella*'s crew couldn't stand the ordeal any longer and decided to go in that cove even if it meant life or death. With sail set on the lifeboat, they sped toward the reef and breakers. They were tossed about, but beached; then managed to crawl over the rocks to the shore in safety.

There were no permanent residents here to take them in; thus they were stranded in nature's worse elements until daylight. The only shelter was the lifeboat sail propped up by two oars. It was hardly big enough to house a dog, but in this crude shelter seven men with wet clothes nearly frozen onto their bodies waited out a cold torrential rain driven by high winds. Exposure soon drained them and several had frost-bitten hands and feet.

At daylight on Thursday, the castaways saw a building in the distance. To reach it they had to walk a virtual obstacle course through bushes, over bog and rock and to make a wide detour up a river until they found a narrow place and shallow water. Eventually they reached a rough hut; a lobster catcher's shack. There was nothing in it to comfort the castaways, a stove but no matches, but at least a roof kept out the weather. Surveying their surroundings, they could see two buildings about a half mile away at Cape Dog on the other side of the bay.

By his time most were too exhausted to go any further; however Captain Green and bosun Harry Russell set out to look for inhabitants. After a day's walk they reached Cape Dog Cove and entered another shack which contained a little food and some hunting equipment. About 7:30 p.m., the man who owned the shack arrived. He had been hunting on the barrens and could guide them to the town of North Harbour, a few miles away, but suggested they wait until morning.

North Harbour, a fishing community located on both sides of a long, narrow inlet of that name, was probably settled in the late 1700s or early 1800s by the Power family, who moved from St. Mary's. The community appears in the first *Census* in 1836 with five families and a total of twenty-two people at North Harbour and Cape Dog. By 1926, when the shipwrecked crew of *Amy Stella* arrived, there were about 150 people at North Harbour, chiefly engaged in the inshore fishery supplemented with small farms. The dominant family names were Power, Bonia, and Ryan.

On that morning when Green and Russell walked to North Harbour, the Bonias, Ryans, and Powers welcomed them into their homes and provided for their material comforts. Two North Harbour men, Peter and John Power, left to look for the remainder of *Amy Stella*'s crew. Carrying food and supplies with them, the Powers walked nine miles through deep snow and over ponds to reach the lobster shack where they lit a fire to warm the shipwrecked men. With hot drink and food, they were soon revived.

By now the heavy seas had abated enough to allow two other men from North Harbour to travel by boat to Big Barachois. The four rescuers were able to retrieve *Amy Stella*'s lifeboat from the rocks and then to guide the remaining shipwrecked men to North Harbour. Eager residents in North Harbour and Colinet opened their homes and hearts, taking the distressed Trinity Bay sailors in. According to the written report of the wreck and rescue:

Four days after shipwreck, on Sunday morning the seamen left for Whitbourne (overland and north for about twenty kilometres) by ponies and catamarans. The people of North Harbour and Colinet turned out to do all they could for them. The party of survivors and rescuers reached Whitbourne at 3 p.m. Sunday and later left for home on the express train. The crew of the ill-fated *Amy Stella* said they would never forget the kindness and open-heartedness of the North Harbour and Colinet people.

The train stopped at Trinity where the men departed to wait until the motor vessel *Seneff* came from Port Union to pick them up. Finally it was over; *Amy Stella*'s crew had high praise for all who helped them in the long journey to Port Union — all except for certain individuals at Trinity. Apparently at Trinity's Garland Hotel they were refused food, but made light of the incident, saying that if they had been wearing white collars, fancy ties, and used a walking stick they would have gotten breakfast.

The Fishermen's Protective Union reviewed their shipping losses over a seven year period: their foreign-going schooner *Nina L.C.* sprang a leak and sank in mid-Atlantic on July 8, 1919. The steamer *Malle de Luxembourg* rescued the crew — Captain Rose, mate G.J. Matthews, bosun Jonathan T. Norman, seamen P. Hiscock, J. Manuel, S. Courage, T. Lodge, and Selby Russell — and carried them to St. Pierre.

Tern schooner *President Coaker* was wrecked near Cape Race in February 1924. All six crew: Captain Norman Sheppard, his brother and mate Harold Sheppard, bosun Alfred Sheppard, and cook George House, all of Port Union and Catalina; John Kelly, Black Duck Cove, Trinity Bay; and Israel Downey, a resident of Port Rexton, were lost. The company also lost three ships wrecked in three months: the *Hillcrest* at Red Island, Placentia Bay, on March 3, 1926, with the death of one sailor (see book *Between Sea and Sky*) and now the foreign-going *Amy Stella*.

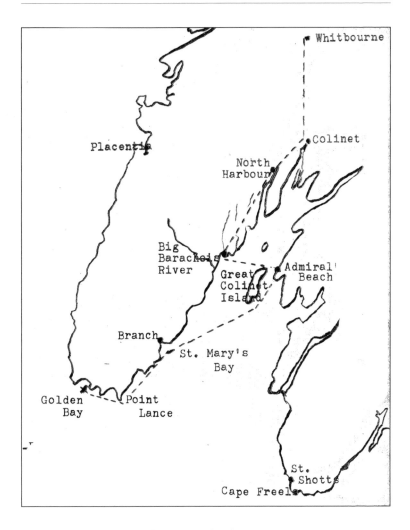

Route of *Amy Stella*'s crew.

Chapter 49

Men of Placentia Bay: Crossing the Atlantic

Harbour Buffett/Merasheen/The Rams/Catalina

In 1917, World War I and the Battle of the Atlantic still raged. Enemy submarines sank shipping, both the merchant fleet and naval ships. Yet Newfoundland schooners continued to ply the trade routes, carrying fish from North America to Europe and often crossing directly into lanes patrolled by German submarines or U-boats. Ever present as well was the tumultuous Atlantic which in the fall of the year, when most foreign-going schooners sailed to Portugal or Spain, was at its stormiest.

So it was on October 22, 1917, when the schooner *Gigantic* left Harbour Buffett, Placentia Bay, for Europe. As it turned out the enemy remained unseen and unheralded, but the six men fought a vicious Atlantic gale which almost did them in.

Gigantic was built in LaHave, Nova Scotia, in 1911. A two-masted schooner netting ninety-nine tons, it was owned by Isaac Wakeley of Harbour Buffett, Placentia Bay. The crew for this particular voyage were Captain Thomas Edgecombe and mate William Edgecombe, both of Catalina, although it is not clear if both men were related. The other four were all from Placentia Bay: cook Wilson Hollett from Harbour Buffett; William Best of Merasheen, a town on the island of Merasheen; William Barry of Port Royal, a town near Harbour Buffett; and Thomas Whiffen lived on the Rams. The Rams, a group of small islands on the eastern side of Placentia Bay, was later renamed Iona. Each of the above mentioned Placentia Bay towns are now abandoned, but in 1917, they were viable and prosperous communities. Seamen from Placentia Bay sailed to many foreign ports and brought back the culture, knowledge, and expertise to their home towns.

Gigantic was no sooner out of port when a fair east northeast wind pushed them along under foresail and two jibs. They rounded Red Island in Placentia Bay and straightened away for Oporto, Portugal. At 8 p.m. they saw the Cape St. Mary's light and gave St. Mary's Keys, a dangerous navigational menace, wide berth.

Wareham's stores and premises in Harbour Buffett c. late 1940s and W. W. Wareham's premises at the height of the salt fish trade: (far left) the roof of the salt bulk storage shed; (foreground) flakes for drying fish; (right) dry fish storage shed in the long white building and (centre) the herring factory.

The next morning, off in the distance and behind them, they saw Cape Pine. Within the next two watches they set the storm sail, checked the log and swung off on the main course for ten hours. On October 24, when about 300 miles from land, a gale came on. Atlantic gales were to be expected and Captain Edgecombe prepared for it. He called out, "All hands on deck. Lower the staysails. You four men — Barry, Best, Hollett, and Whiffen — go aloft and reef the foresail and storm sail."

Edgecombe had his ship "hove to" as wind intensity increased. By now *Gigantic* was taking waves across its deck; one particularly large comber struck the lifeboat and split it apart.

For twenty-eight hours, at the western edge of the Gulf Stream, the schooner lay to, making little forward progress in the face of strong and adverse winds. One of the sailors said, "the winds and seas the like you seldom seen. We young boys will never forget the seas that rolled down that night."

To make matters worse, *Gigantic* became leaky from the severe pounding. Every man pumped round the clock, 300 strokes an hour. On October 31, the storm peaked. The schooner lay to under a double-reefed foresail with all crew on deck, trying to keep the schooner afloat.

Although there is no known photo of *Gigantic*, this sailing ship the *Samoset* (above) probably sailed the Atlantic from a Placentia Bay port in 1917 as did the *Gigantic*.

Built in Gloucester in 1898, the fifty-eight foot long schooner *Samoset* was sold to Abraham Street of Burin in 1912, passed to George Rodway of Harbour Buffett and finally to John R. Rodway of Baine Harbour in 1949. Sometime in the 1950s the old *Samoset* was pulled onto a beach at Baine Harbour to die.

In this photo the schooner is moored in the bottom at Baine Harbour near Watering Brook, a place where schooners replenished their supply of water. Photo courtesy Annie Collett, Baine Harbour.

But just as quickly as it came on, the storm disapated. On November 1, the sea was calm. In good time they reached Portugal and the experience of Captain Edgecombe and his crew kept the vessel right on course. The first sign of human life was the Oporto harbour tug which stood offshore and blew its whistle on their approach.

After twenty-three days, the six reached port and were delighted to furl sails, wash down the deck, and make general repairs to their beleaguered schooner. With a regular watch, they soon caught up on sleep. The load of fish was discharged five miles up the Duro River which runs through Oporto. After *Gigantic* took on a load of salt, the well-rested crew headed home.

Seen above harboured at Petite Forte, the schooner *M & J Hayden*, of twenty-eight net tons and built in 1926 at St. Joseph's, Placentia Bay, for Joseph Hayden, was eventually sold to William King, Deer Harbour, Trinity Bay. For eight years it was commanded by Captain Jim Harris of St. Joseph's.

On September 27, 1930, Captain James Hayden and Peter Murphy of *M. & J. Hayden* witnessed the collision between the Burin schooner *Vibert Shave* and the steamer *Haugerland*, but could not warn either ship in time to prevent the accident. Five of the six crew on *Vibert Shave* were lost.

Conditions were better on the westward voyage; ship and sailors arrived without incident. *Gigantic* didn't last long after that. In November 1919 it sprang a leak and was abandoned in the Atlantic — the crew was picked up by the steamer *Craigsmere* and taken to New York.

Not all ships beating the Atlantic that fall were as lucky as *Gigantic*. The *Creusa G*, a two-masted vessel owned in St. Lawrence, left port to get coal at Sydney. It never reported in St. Lawrence and it is thought that during the storm of November 9, 1917, it went down. Lost were five St. Lawrence men: Robert Fitzpatrick, age thirty-six; David Fitzpatrick, forty-nine; Joseph Fitzpatrick, twenty-three; Robert Pike, twenty-four; and Robert Slaney, thirty-eight.

Chapter 50

Battling Plague and Storm

In the fall of 1923, Captain Hollett sailed from Burin to Oporto. Competent and knowledgeable captains like Hollett regularly made the 3,000 mile journey to deliver salt dry fish to Portugal and Greece and to return with fishery salt to cure the fish. Hollett's ship was the two-masted *Annie M. Parker*, laden with fish. Of the other five crew who, most likely, were from Burin and area only the names of Wilson Hoben, the cook, and Captain Hollett have been recorded.

Hollett had a fine trip eastward, all crew was in good health and, after the fish was discharged and *Annie M. Parker* had the cargo of salt in the hold, the ship left Portugal. Eleven days out circumstances changed.

The mate suddenly became ill with smallpox contracted in Portugal. Captain Hollett and the rest of the crew did everything in their power to ease the sick man's suffering. On board a foreign-going schooner, there was limited means to cure sickness and the mate's condition became progressively worse.

Twenty-eight days after leaving Oporto, Captain Hollett sighted Cape Race. Hopes of getting the dying man to land immediately rose and it looked like his life would be saved. But nature intervened. Shortly after Hollett sighted land, a strong northeast gale pounced directly in their face and prevented any easy trip to a Newfoundland port. In fact, the storm dismasted the ship and blew it far out to sea.

Burin c. 1920-30s. In the background is Great Burin Island; now abandoned but was once a thriving community. In the foreground are the walkways and bridges to the village of Shalloway. Burin was one of the leading Newfoundland towns in the bank fishing era and had a large fleet of schooners.

Annie M. Parker began to leak and the storm left it a drifting, helpless hulk. Aboard was a man close to death with smallpox. Two days later, an eastbound Dutch steamer sighted the schooner and plucked off the five crew, including the sick mate. *Annie M. Parker*, abandoned and with no one to man the pumps, sank within a few hours.

Three days after rescue, the mate passed away and was buried at sea; the remaining four men were put in isolation and quarantined aboard the steamer. By the time they arrived in Amsterdam, three more of *Annie M. Parker*'s crew became seriously ill with smallpox and were rushed to hospital.

In the 1920s, smallpox, a viral and highly contagious disease, was nearly always fatal. The acute illness lasted about three weeks and should the person, through some unknown reserves of strength, recover convalescence lasted another two to three weeks. Today smallpox has nearly been eradicated.

Tern schooner *General Maude* (above), owned by the Marystown Trading Company, operated out of Marystown for many years. Seaman John Stapleton of Marystown recorded his experiences on one foreign-going trip.

In the spring of 1919, *General Maude* left Marystown with a load of salt cod to be discharged at Bari, Italy — its crew: Captain George Hickman, John and Joe Stapleton, Ernie Brake, and Patrick Barry. Captain Hickman was from Grand Bank, while the other four were from Marystown and area.

The eastward voyage took twelve days and when the fish was discharged in Italy, the vessel received a "pass" to proceed to Gibraltar for further orders. Before *General Maude* left Europe, it loaded salt for Marystown. Head winds of July and August made the return voyage longer and more difficult, but in seventy-eight days it arrived. The long voyage reduced food supplies severely; the crew had no bread, coffee or beans, but plenty of cod liver oil and salt pork.

Another instance of *General Maude*'s activities can be found in the log book of the harbour authority at Bridgewater, Nova Scotia. On September 23, 1924, register it states: Tern schooner *General Maude*, 140 tons, hailing from St. John's. Captain Rose from Lockeport, Nova Scotia, bound to Bridgewater to load lumber for Cuba. Pilotage ten dollars.

General Maude was abandoned in the Atlantic on March 26, 1926; Captain Hickman and crew were rescued by a passing steamer. Photo courtesy of Shelburne County Museum.

Hollett and cook Hoben, who showed no sign of smallpox, were placed in quarantine as a precaution, but were released when they were declared free from sickness. Dutch authorities found the two a passage to Liverpool, England, but they left three sick comrades behind. By this time the Christmas season had come and gone. All the

Newfoundland seamen had experienced so far was a battle with the treacherous Atlantic, their ship gone, sickness, the death of one shipmate, and a festive season spent in a foreign land far from home.

Hollett and Hoben came across the Atlantic on the Cunard liner *Ansonia*, arriving in Halifax in early February 1924. They went to North Sydney and met with A.W. (Arthur William) Shano. He was born in Lower Island Cove, Newfoundland, worked in various Newfoundland post offices and had recently been promoted to head up the Newfoundland branch of the Postal Department at North Sydney. On February 20, Shano arranged a passage to Newfoundland on the S.S. *Kyle*. While in Nova Scotia, Captain Hollett visited his cousin, L. Hollett, living in Sydney Mines.

Lucy Melinda (above), built by Daniel Kelly as a fishing vessel at Little Bay, Placentia Bay, for John Power and named after Power's two daughters. It was converted to a coasting schooner in 1951.

In this photo taken November 11, 1955, it lies aground at Cannon Point in the mouth of St. Pierre harbour with the lighthouse to the right. The crew at this time was Captain Gus Power, Tom Walsh, Tom Murphy, and Peter Poulain of Little Bay.

Eventually *Lucy Melinda* was refloated by French salvors, repaired and renamed *Cap Perce*. On September 5, 1958, it sank off St. Pierre laden with Sydney coal.

Two months had passed since Captain Hollett and his crew left Burin for a voyage to Portugal. Eventually the remaining three men returned home from Amsterdam.

Chapter 51

When Debris Drifts Ashore: Loss of the Ravenel

The discovery of a life belt and part of a vessel's hatch cover near Lories-Point May on February 1 and 2, 1962, confirmed the worst fears. But there was no sea mystery to be solved. Everyone in the general area knew a ship had been overdue for several days. The life belt with the word 'RAVENEL' inscribed was from the deep sea dragger *Ravenel* of St. Pierre.

Lories, located at the tip of the Burin Peninsula and the closest Newfoundland town to the French Islands, like other south coast communities had been buffeted by a severe winter gale. January and February are trying months for deep sea fishing off Newfoundland — storms and high seas are more common during those months and fish laden draggers put up a tremendous battle with the elements to survive. Hurricane force winds didn't stop landsmen of Lories and Point May from combing the shores especially a beach near Flagstaff as they looked for any evidence of the missing ship that might have drifted ashore.

Built in France a year earlier, and a sister ship to the dragger *Savoyard*, *Ravenel* was captained by Jacob Thornhill of Grand Bank up to December 1961. It was then that Captain Fily took command. He and his crew had been fishing for several days in late January. According to printed sources, Fily had taken nearly a full load, but there are those on St. Pierre today who believe the vessel was nearly empty. If so, that certainly would make *Ravenel* more unstable.

One thing is certain; there had been high winds and heavy seas. This increased the chances that the vessel would "ice up" or become coated with a layer of ice from the freezing spray. Layers of thick ice changes a ship's centre of gravity, decreases stability and makes the possibility of it listing out on one side or rolling over.

Owned by the fish company at St. Pierre, SPEC, (Societé De Pêche Et De Congélation), *Ravenel* disappeared near St. Pierre in late January 1962. Fifteen men were lost with the vessel. Photo courtesy of Briand Ozon Photography Studio, St. Pierre via Ben Stacey, Point May/Grand Bank.

Captain Adrien Fily radioed St. Pierre at 2:15 p.m. on Saturday, January 27, to say he was headed home from the Grand Banks. He also said he planned to stop on the St. Pierre Banks — about 100 miles from the French Islands — to make a few more tows over those productive grounds. It is not clear if Captain Fily indicated *Ravenel* had iced up or if it was having difficulty in the high seas. On January 30, fish plant personnel tried to make contact, but could not. Often during high winds or freezing spray, radio antennas broke or iced up and ships were not able to send or receive messages.

From the point of the captain's contact with shore on Saturday, there was silence, an ominous silence. *Ravenel* should have been in port by this time. Within a day or two a sea search failed to find the dragger. The RCMP cutter *Wood* and the Department of Transport icebreaker *Wolf* scoured the seas off St. Pierre. Winds hampered an aerial search, but by Thursday February 1, RCAF search and rescue planes and a Neptune aircraft from the US Naval Station at Argentia had covered over 20,000 square miles with no sighting of the missing ship.

Speculation held that *Ravenel* probably hit the treacherous reefs off the southern tip of the Burin Peninsula. Since it was well laden with fish and probably ice covered, the chances for survival were low if the vessel hit a reef or underwater rocks. Land search parties under the supervision of the RCMP combed the shores of the Burin Peninsula and with the discovery of wreckage at High Beach near Lories from *Ravenel*, its loss was confirmed.

A few days later, a wheelhouse door and a boot identified as belonging to a crew member drifted in on Lories' beach. It is said that in the fall of 1964, the bell from the bridge of *Ravenel* was found on the beach of Green Island near St. Pierre, but this seems impossible. A heavy metal bell was usually welded or bolted onto the

---

THE SONG OF THE *RAVENEL*, MISSING SINCE JANUARY 1962

Come all ye hearty fishermen,
Come listen to my tale
About a fine French trawler
Her name, the *Ravenel*.

She left St. Pierre with fifteen men
For the Grand Banks she did sail
No one knew she would never return,
The ship, the *Ravenel*.

They had a very fine skipper
And a very fine crew likewise,
Some were lately married
Who went and left their wives.

The twenty-seventh of January
The owners they did hear
For they were sailing for their homes
And loved ones at St. Pierre...

Written by the late singer/song writer Gabriel Parsons Sr. of Point May who lost a nephew on the *Ravenel*. These are the first four verses of a thirteen verse song.

steel superstructure on or near the bridge. The likelihood of this floating or drifting ashore is remote. The exact position of where the dragger went down has never been definitely determined.

All crew were from the French Islands — St. Pierrais: Captain Fily, André Urdanabia, Charles Poulard, Yvon Poulard, Roger Renou, Henri Lahiton, Joseph Bonnieul, Lionel Rebmann, Eugène Claireaux, Amédée Revert, Gérard Autin, Frédéric Olano, Robert Bourgeois, Jean LaFargue, and Jean Orsiny. Many of these men were married with families; fifty-three children were left fatherless.

Often too Point May girls married the young men of St. Pierre. Many years before Adele Parsons and her two sisters of Point May married St. Pierrais. Adele married a Revert whose son, Amédée, was lost and thus the tragedy affected Newfoundland families, friends, and cousins directly.

St. Pierre-Miquelon (SPM) dragger *Galantry* moored at St. Pierre. Note the mooring bollard formed from an old cannon. *Galantry*, built in Holland in 1954, was the oldest trawler in SPM's fleet. While fishing on St. Pierre Bank on October 30, 1962, a heavy door which held the mouth of the otter trawl open, hit the side of the dragger. It gashed the steel plate below the waterline, pumps could not contain the inflow and with a few hours *Galantry* went down. Fortunately the crew was able to SOS a Canadian vessel nearby which came to the rescue. Photo courtesy of the late Fred Tessier, Grand Bank.

As is the case with local traumatic events, the singer/songwriter penned a song on the event. The late Gabriel Parsons, whose sister's son was lost, composed thirteen verses in "The Song of the *Ravenel*" and put his own air or tune to it. Now the song — the first four verses are given here — is a popular come-all-ye.

Chapter 52

Fire at Sea

ire at sea! To sailors shipboard explosions and fire
represents one of the most dangerous situations that
can happen on board a ship. Often they have no time
to signal for help; valuable time is taken fighting the blaze
or preparing to launch a lifeboat. The forward movement
of the ship will fan any flames on deck or if the fire is
below, heat and smoke prevent ready access to a confined
engine room or hold to fight the flames.

During one week in August 1948, no less than three
ships were racked by spectacular explosions and fires
while off Nova Scotia — two in less than forty-eight
hours. On August 12, the *Ronnie F* of Lunenburg exploded and sank. Its three crew from Lunenburg rowed to
shore.

Less than a day later, news reached shipping authori-
ties that another ship had exploded and burned at South
Bar near Sydney. The 105 foot long *Ernest G*, a converted
navy Fairmile hauling coal, gasoline, and motor fuel to
Newfoundland, was registered to Albert Griffin of
Montague, Prince Edward Island. It was crewed by
Newfoundlanders: Captain George Douglas, age sixty-
four; his eighteen-year-old son Fred; engineer George
Snook; cook Charles Thomas, all of Grand Bank; and
mate George P. Elford of Fortune.

Captain Douglas, a knowledgeable and veteran skipper said the fire broke out while the ship was almost opposite the lighthouse about forty-five minutes out of North Sydney. Douglas thought the blaze started with oil splashed out around the diesel engines. He reported:

> Engineer George Snook emptied the contents of two fire extinguishers on the flames but could not contain the fire. There was so much heat that Snook could not reach the throttle after I called to him to stop the engines. It was impossible for him to do so.

True to his learned experiences and the traditions of the sea, Captain Douglas remained at the wheel until the flame-spouting craft hit the sand barrier on South Bar, located about seven miles from Sydney. Before that he had ordered his four crew into the dory. After Douglas had directed his flaming ship away from the sea lanes, his crew came alongside in the dory and Captain Douglas joined them. Douglas said:

> There was less than fifteen minutes between my 'Get the hell off this!' order and the first explosion. The crew was rowing around in the smoke for about fifteen minutes before I joined them. *Ernest G* hit the sandbar about 3,000 yards from shore and then I got in the dory. I had made fourteen trips in that ship before now.
>
> We were picked up by the RCMP harbour craft *Brule* and taken back to North Sydney.

Headlines on August 20, 1948, from *The Halifax Herald*, after the trawler *Arleux* exploded and sank in three minutes. Two other ships were destroyed by fire and explosions off Nova Scotia less than a week previously.

Ernest G was full of combustible material. It had arrived in North Sydney in early August to load coal. Other cargo included two barrels of gasoline and 1,500 gallons of fuel oil. The extent of the ensuing explosions were best described by the South Bar lighthouse keeper George MacLean:

> It was a spectacular fire display at night. There were two explosions which sent flames far into the sky. Flames and smoke were shooting in the air. You could see the shoreline all around. The heat was terrific and smoke cut off the view but I could see the ship was blazing near the waterline.
>
> The derelict ended up stranded about 300 feet from the lighthouse, lying on its side in the sand — its last resting place.

On August 19, 1948, the Halifax trawler *Arleux* (above) exploded fifteen miles off Whitehead Bay, Nova Scotia, and sank. Nine of its twenty-two crew were from Newfoundland: William Grant, Fortune; Garfield Drake, Lally Cove; William Quann, Harbour Breton; William Phillips, Hare Harbour or Belleoram; Charles Handcock, Pool's Cove; Randell Pink, Rose Blanche; and three from Burin, Daniel Doody, James Whalen and Cyril Mills. Photo courtesy of Hubert Hall, SHIPSEARCH (Marine), Yarmouth, Nova Scotia.

Emily H. Patten (above) was built at McKay Yards, Shelburne. It netted 152 tons and was 108 feet long. This is a photo painted by the waterfront artists of Portugal. When a North American sailing ship docked in Oporto, an artist sketched the ship. Often the captain would purchase the painting; the artist made a few dollars and a piece of Newfoundland history was captured on canvas for posterity. Photo courtesy of Susan Hodgson, Union, Ohio, via Frank Patten, Ontario.

The Daily News of February 4, 1929, recorded the event of the loss of another fine tern schooner, *Emily H. Patten*. When abandoned in a sinking condition on February 1, 1929, its crew was: Captain Hughie Grandy, Robert Harris, William Keating, John Grandy, George Hatcher, and cook Augusta Almeda. All were from Grand Bank except Almeda who was born in Portugal. He came to Grand Bank on a foreign-going schooner to begin a new life in Newfoundland.

> Author's note: Several years ago I asked an older gentleman, Clarence Griffen of Grand Bank, if he knew anything about the schooner *Emily H. Patten* or its wreck. Clarence told me weeks before any news of its loss came back to Grand Bank, he had a dream about the abandonment of *Emily H. Patten* in mid-ocean. It was so real he could see the movements and the preparations of the crew as they were about to leave ship and climb into the waiting lifeboat.
>
> When Augusta Almeda arrived home, Griffen described to him how he and the other crew got into the lifeboat on the port side, what they were wearing, and so on. Almeda confirmed that it was exactly how it happened.

SOURCES

NEWSPAPERS

Catholic Herald
Courier
Daily News
Moncton Daily Times
Evening Herald
Evening Telegram
Family Fireside
Fisherman's Advocate
Halifax Chronicle-Herald

Harbour Grace Standard
Mail and Advocate
Morning Chronicle
National Geographic
Patriot
St. John's Times
Sydney Post
Trade Review
Western Star

PUBLICATIONS

Best, Anita and G. Lear. *Come and I Will Sing You*, Breakwater, 1985.

Canadian Coast Guard. *Shipping Casualties off Canada's Atlantic Coast 1896-1980.*

Parker, John. *Sails of the Maritimes*. McGraw-Hill Ryerson, 1960.

Peacock, Kenneth. *Songs of Newfoundland's Outports*. National Museum of Canada, 1965.

ARCHIVES, MUSEUMS AND PERSONAL COLLECTIONS

A.C. Hunter Library, Newfoundland Reference Room, St. John's, NL.

CNS, Memorial University of Newfoundland, St. John's, NL.

Dept. Natural Resources, Surveys and Mapping Division, St. John's, NL.

Maritime History Archives, Memorial University, St. John's, NL.

Public Archives of Nova Scotia, Halifax, NS.

Pouch Cove Museum and Town Hall, NL.

Public Archives of Nova Scotia, Halifax, NS.

Ship photos Capt. H. Hall, SHIPSEARCH (Marine) Yarmouth, NS.
Ship statistics and expertise, Jack Keeping, Fortune, NL.
Shelburne County Museum, Shelburne, NS.
Trepassey Town Library, NL.
United States National Archives, Washington, USA.

I AM GRATEFUL FOR PERSONAL CORRESPONDENCE AND/OR PHOTOS FROM THESE PEOPLE:

Stewart Abbott, Gander, formerly of Musgrave Harbour, NL.
Gerald Adams, St. John's, NL.
Ron Barbour, ?, NL.
Harold Batstone, Jackson's Cove, NL.
Don Blackmore, Bloomfield, NL, formerly of Port Union, NL.
Lance Blackmore Grand Bank, NL, formerly of Port Union, NL.
Bud and Olive Boyce, Marystown, NL.
Bursell Bragg, Pouch Cove, NL.
Ralph Brown, Lewisporte, NL.
Captain William Brushett, Burin, NL.
Doug Burgess, Billtown, NS.
Hayward Burry, Glovertown, NL.
Marion (Smith) Carson, Montreal, QC, formerly of Conception Bay, NL.
Norman Chaytor, St. John's, NL.
Conrad Clarke, North Sydney, NS.
Ralph Clemens, St. John's, NL.
The late Rev. V. Cluett, Nova Scotia/Belleoram, NL.
Annie Collett, Baine Harbour, NL.
Ricky Corrigan, Trepassey, NL.
Garry Crewe, St. John's, NL.
Jeannie Cunningham, Tucson, Arizona.
Emma Currie, Clarenville, NL.
Don Doliber ?
Ena Farrell Edwards, St. Lawrence, NL.
Barbara (Bennett) Esposito, East Haven, Connecticut.
John Ford, St. John's, NL, formerly of Port aux Basques, NL.
Llewellyn Grimes, Herring Neck, NL.
Jack Hackett, Terrenceville, NL.

Rae Hadley, Halifax, NS.

Susan Hodgson, Union, Ohio.

Domino House, Hare Bay/St. John's, NL.

Steen Jorgensen, Edmonton, AB.

Gordon King, St. John's, NL.

Andre LaFargue, Saint John, NB, formerly of St. Pierre.

Denis Lahiton, Fortune, NL, formerly of St. Pierre.

Jessie Mercer, Shearstown, NL.

Dave Morrissey, St. John's, NL.

Lizetta Murphy, Marystown, NL.

Bruce Musson, formerly of Port aux Basques, NL.

Bruce Neal, St. John's, NL.

Eric Norenius, Port Hope, ON.

Franklyn Noseworthy, Pouch Cove, NL.

Enid O'Brien, Cape Broyle, NL.

Nelson Oram, Glovertown, NL.

Gabriel Parsons, Fortune, NL, formerly of Point May, NL.

Mona Petten, Port-de-Grave, NL.

Dave Piercey, Fortune, NL.

Captain Joe Prim, St. John's, NL.

Stella Roberts, Baie d'Espoir, NL.

Robert Smith, Victoria Harbour, ON.

Calvin and Margaret Snow, Carbonear, NL.

Mike Snow, New Hampshire.

Richard Spracklin, Edmonton, AB.

Ben Stacey, Grand Bank, NL, formerly of Point May, NL.

Joe Stapleton, Marystown, NL.

Harry Stone, St. John's, NL.

Gordon Stoodley, Harbour Breton, NL.

Rennie Sullivan, Pouch Cove, NL.

The late Frederick Tessier, Grand Bank, NL.

Herb Thomasen, St. Catherines, ON, formerly of Grand Bank, NL.

Wayne Timbury ?

Clarence Vautier, St. John's, NL, formerly of LaPoile, NL.

Doug Wells, Harbour Breton, NL.

INDEX OF VESSELS, TOWNS, AND LANDMARKS

Vienna 10
Viking 46
Virginia 187

W

Wadham Islands 12
Walter Kennedy
151, 152, 153
Waterwitch 164-170
W.C. McKay 183
Wesleyville 52, 76,
82, 87, 89, 96, 98,
147, 181, 187
Western Bay 59, 60,
143
Western Bay Point
59
W.G. Robertson 99
Windsor Lake 189
Winnie Pierce 12
Winterton 199-200
Witless Bay 220
Wolf 241
Wood 241
Wood's Island 39
Woody Island 11
Wop 149-153
Wren 151, 153

Y

Yarmouth, NS 174

INDEX OF PERSONS AND BUSINESSES
* THE NAMES IN BOLD WERE THOSE LOST AT SEA

OTHER BOOKS AVAILABLE BY ROBERT PARSONS

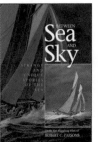

BETWEEN SEA AND SKY:
Strange and Unique Stories of the Sea (2002)
ISBN 1-894294-43-2
5.5 x 8.5, 300 pages
paper — $17.95

At the extreme extent of our vision, the sea and sky merge together, becoming only a line on the horizon. Sailors and fishers exist in a fragile, self-contained world — the ship — which serves to separate sea and sky.

Ever subject to the elements of weather, wind and sea, these individuals, particularly in times past, survived through their skill and knowledge, coupled with a propensity for hard work under trying circumstances. That so many survived is a testament to that skill and knowledge; when skill and knowledge weren't sufficient, survival usually became a matter of good luck.

RAGING WINDS . . .
ROARING SEA (2000)
(Second printing December 2001)
ISBN 1-894294-29-7
5.5 x 8.5, 200 pages
paper — $16.95

Raging Winds ... Roaring Sea is about people and the sea. This book tells for the first time stories of little-known shipping disasters that occurred along Newfoundland and Labrador coasts. These tales of the sea cross time and shorelines to bring to life the names, the people, the towns and the ships. Here Robert Parsons brings to the printed page many of the mysteries and shipwrecks that have puzzled and fascinated people for years. Stories in this collection go beyond the marine misadventure to feature the people, the descendants and the lives touched by hardship.

LOST AT SEA — A Compilation (2001)

ISBN 1-894294-34-3
5.5 x 8.5, 312 pages
paper — $19.95

The Grand Banks of Newfoundland were once the most prolific fishing grounds in the world. Ships and men from many countries harvested its bounty, but none were more courageous or industrious than Newfoundland's own fishermen. Although the fishing grounds were generous, the sea itself was, and is, unforgiving. Many ships and crew failed to return after a season's fishing, and only brief newspaper articles remain to report their fate. In the late 1980s Robert Parsons began researching these stories, fleshing out the brief newspaper accounts with personal memories garnered from the few remaining fishermen who had fished the Grand Banks in open dories. Originally published in 1991 and 1992 in two volumes, *Lost at Sea* is being brought back due to popular demand, and has been compiled into one volume. This new release contains the complete text, photographs and illustrations contained in the original two books. The stories cover the roughly one hundred year period from the late 1860s to the early 1970s, and tell of shipwrecks and marine disasters involving ships and crews from Newfoundland's South Coast fishing communities.

COMMITTED TO THE DEEP: Stories and Memoirs (1999)

ISBN 1-894294-09-2
5.5 x 8.5, 288 pages
paper — $16.95

Committed to the Deep is a collection of thirty-nine thrilling sea tales as told by those who lived them. Read first-person accounts, yarns and anecdotes about collisions at sea, lighthouses, mid-ocean rescues, disappearances, a woman's heroics, and much more. Robert Parsons has produced another volume of unique and fascinating sea stories which will be enjoyed by all those who love the moody sea.

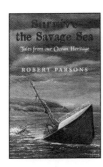

SURVIVE THE SAVAGE SEA: Tales From Our Ocean Heritage (1998)

(Fourth printing August 2002)
ISBN 1-895387-96-5
5.5 x 8.5, 300 pages
paper — $19.95

Shipwrecks have been a fact of life and death as long as men have sailed the oceans. The marine disasters that have occurred around Newfoundland's shores since John Cabot's time have been many; just how many may never be known. Recently, the late historian Keith Matthews and Captain Joe Prim estimated 10,000 to 15,000 vessels have been lost on or near Newfoundland and Labrador. Professor Thomas Nemec has focused on one area, the southern end of the Avalon Peninsula, and documented more than 300 shipwrecks in that location. White's Newfoundland shipwreck map shows scores of ship losses which happened prior to 1903.

Yet, the sea is still in our blood. There is scarcely a Newfoundlander today who cannot trace his or her roots to a schooner owner, captain, seaman or bank fisherman. Newfoundland schooners and our forefathers who sailed them laid down the designs of settlement and the protocols of island trade that gave Newfoundland its present culture.

This book takes us around the island clockwise beginning on the west coast and ending near Cape Ray, and covers a period roughly of one hundred years. Each story (of around 130 ships) within these covers is true; however, all are subject to the vagaries of human memory and fallibility of newspaper reporters.

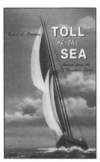

TOLL OF THE SEA: Stories From the Forgotten Coast (1995)
(Second printing February 2002)
ISBN 1-895387-51-5
5.5 x 8.5, 244 pages
paper — $14.95

Toll of the Sea tells of the communities along Newfoundland's South Coast, often referred to in yesteryear's print as 'The Forgotten Coast.' Away from the mainstream Avalon Peninsula and the more populous northeast corner of the island, this economically stable area was busy at the turn of the century sending schooners to the banks and tern schooners to foreign markets, but South Coast communities paid a price in lost ships and men.

VIGNETTES OF A SMALL TOWN (1997)
ISBN 1-895387-82-5
5.5 x 8.5, 320 pages
paper — $19.95

Grand Bank, Newfoundland, was for many years the hub of Newfoundland's offshore fishery. It is a town of solidly built houses, and strong family values. In this book Parsons provides a capsule history of this typical working class town and its people, their lives and accomplishments.